Adventures in Travel

Stories of Perils, Pitfalls and Mishaps Around the World

By Brian Borgford

ISBN: 1507779941
ISBN 13: 9781507779941

Introduction

With well over sixty years of life behind me, I have had the opportunity to travel the world. In addition to living in several regions of Canada, I have lived in China, the United Arab Emirates, and Qatar. I have also been able to visit many countries in Europe, Asia, and Africa. Years of travel tend to yield some interesting experiences, and this book is meant to share some of my more memorable travel stories. Although I have many others, most of them, however enjoyable, do not evoke the emotional experiences of those adventures contained herein.

The sequence of the stories is in the order of what I felt was interesting and exciting with the more adventurous stories early in the book and the less exciting stories toward the end.

The majority of my travels have occurred since my marriage to Rochelle, whom you will see has recounted many of the stories first-hand, when she was the principal person affected. However, you will also notice references to my first wife, Marlene, with whom I have maintained a strong friendship since our divorce many years ago.

Please enjoy our travel stories, and feel free to send your comments to me or post a review on Amazon.com or on Goodreads.com.

Brian Borgford, author

brianborgford@hotmail.com

Other related books:

Living in China: Our Year in Shenyang

Rochelle

From Couch Potato to Weekend Athlete

Fear

This section is devoted to those incidents that created fear or anxiety during the travel experience. Sometimes it was fear for physical well-being, and other times it was fear of losing sanity. Either way, they represent significant emotional experiences.

K...K...Karachi

May 2011

One of my rare dozes on an airplane was interrupted by an announcement from the pilot.

"We have a small technical problem and will be landing at the nearest airport. We do apologize for any inconvenience."

Inconvenience couldn't begin to describe the next twenty-four hours. It was May Day—the first of May, which originated from the French prophetic word *m'aider*, which means "help me." Look the up May 1, 2011 on Google.

We were less than ninety minutes into our flight from Doha to Phuket where Rochelle and I were looking forward to a relaxing week on the beach. However, the first leg of our trip took us on an unexpected adventure.

The nearest airport, according to the pilot's next announcement, was Karachi, Pakistan. Did he say Karachi?

My first thought was, "Why would a small technical problem warrant a stop in a third-world terrorist country that is on the top of most 'don't travel there' lists?"

The Canadian government stated on their website:

Foreign Affairs, Trade and Development Canada advises against non-essential travel to Pakistan due

to the unpredictable security situation and the threat of terrorist attacks.

The US government's travel website was even more frightening in their depiction of our destination:

The presence of several foreign and indigenous terrorist groups poses a potential danger to US citizens throughout Pakistan. Across the country, terrorist attacks frequently occur against civilian, government, and foreign targets. Attacks have included armed assaults on heavily guarded sites, including Pakistani military installations. The government of Pakistan maintains heightened security measures, particularly in the major cities. Threat reporting indicates terrorist groups continue to seek opportunities to attack locations where US citizens and westerners are known to congregate or visit. Terrorists and criminal groups regularly resort to kidnapping for ransom.

This didn't sound good. After a smooth, uneventful landing, our plane halted on a remote runway with no buildings or civilization in sight. A flight attendant barked through the speakers for us to disembark the plane as quickly as possible and not to take any of our hand luggage with us. Rochelle and I both grabbed our carry-on bags, and in spite of protests from the attendants, we marched passed them with our bags in hand. I wasn't prepared to leave my computer and other assorted electronics as salvage for whomever might get on the plane next.

We were among the first passengers off the plane and into the intense heat and humidity of our unexpected destination. The attendants almost pushed people from the plane, as if it were about to explode or be consumed by flames. We hopped onto a waiting bus. The tarmac and surrounding area were filled with military and emergency vehicles, as well as an ambulance, lots of well-armed soldiers, and police. As our stifling non-air-conditioned bus pulled away from the plane, we could see the remaining passengers being hustled off to a field away from the runway, standing in the baking sun and awaiting the return of the only bus available to transport them.

I was sure I could see liquid pouring from the underside of the plane on the tarmac below. I thought, "Fuel," but no one was talking.

The crowded, hot, sticky bus—which could have passed as an import from Cuba, given its age and state of repair—took almost twenty minutes to reach the Jinnah International Airport terminal. Our Qatar Airways attendants were nowhere in sight when we slipped off the bus and into the terminal. We were at the mercy of local officials, many of whom wore uniforms, had bushy beards, and carried weapons that looked like they could eliminate the entire western world-none spoke any English.

The officials demanded that we turn in our boarding passes. Fortunately, I had ours with me due to our belligerence in carrying our hand luggage. I'm not sure how the others who left theirs on the plane skated through this request. I protested as our passes contained our baggage tags, but the menacing attendants assured me that they would return our passes when we handed in the laminated cards we were given in exchange. What choice did I have?

Armed guards monitored our every move as local attendants ushered their unwelcome guests through a security screening process that rivaled any American airport. Women were separated from the men as each gender had its own screening area and process. I was relieved to join up with Rochelle when we and three hundred-some passengers entered the main part of the terminal.

Locals then ushered us into a waiting area where we sat with no food or drink and no communication from anyone as to what was happening or when we might expect to leave. We were able to wander short distances for washrooms and snacks, but wandering beyond that was met with an armed guard and a scowl.

Our US cash was gratefully accepted in exchange for water, chips, and chocolate bars. Again, we just sat as the clocked ticked away. No one got upset or angry—perhaps because of the presence of so many armed guards. We felt like we were being held hostage.

We sat in this cordoned off area for almost two hours before a local Qatar Airways representative showed up with some stale sandwiches accompanied by chocolate wafers and some lukewarm, presweetened tea already mixed with milk.

Now into our third hour with no inkling as to what was happening and what was next, it was becoming quite clear we weren't leaving Karachi soon. By 10:00 a.m. local time, almost four hours into our ordeal, another Qatar Airways representative announced to the few that could hear him that we would meet downstairs in half an hour and buses would take us to the airplane to retrieve our hand luggage. As we already had our hand luggage, I contemplated not going but decided it would be best to stay with the pack. Good choice as it turned out.

The half hour turned into almost two hours—bringing us to six hours at the Karachi airport. Then, we were finally led down to waiting buses, again with no air conditioning, in the hot, humid air. We drove the twenty minutes to our A330, which was still sitting on a remote part of the runway system surrounded by military personnel with frightening weapons in hand. All of the luggage from our flight was lined up about a hundred meters from the plane on the tarmac.

The stern-looking soldiers stood guard outside our bus and insisted that only five passengers at a time could exit to locate their luggage. The rest of us sat sweltering on the bus awaiting our turns. When we finally got our turn, we waltzed up and down the aisles of checked luggage under the watchful eye of the armed guards until we were able to locate ours and point to it. But they didn't allow us to take it away; they just chalk marked our bags with an X and sent us back toward the bus. By now it was apparent that they were allowing passengers to climb the stairs of the plane, again five at a time, to retrieve their hand luggage. We didn't need to retrieve our bags, but we still decided to follow suit. The guards would not let us walk the one hundred meters to the plane; instead, they forced us to back on the bus in order to drive to the airplane.

We went through the motions of retrieving the bags that were actually in our hands already and then descended the stairs to re-enter the sweltering bus for the drive back to the terminal.

Now people were getting very upset with the lack of air conditioning on the bus and pounded on the glass partition to get the driver to at least leave the door open for some air movement. One of the passengers who had not yet gotten on the bus started to clutch his chest in agony while others came to his aid. It looked like he was having heart attack in the hot, humid, stressful environment. People tended to him on the ground as our bus pulled away. Seeing the gentleman later in the day confirmed that his condition was not serious.

Once back at the terminal, we again had to go through the same security process as before. Then we were shown back to our seats to await more of the rare communication from what was now becoming a very negligent airline.

After another long wait, we heard, more through rumour than announcement, that we would be taken to a hotel until the problem was fixed—possibly by 9:30 p.m. that night. It was now almost 1:00 p.m., well past our planned arrival time in Phuket. Not knowing how long this next process would take, Rochelle and I decided to go to a McDonald's we had seen in the terminal to share a burger and fries. We ordered the meal but were informed that it would take over half an hour because they don't make the food there; they bring the orders in from outside. Cancel that idea—we didn't know if we had enough time before our next move. So we just ordered some drinks with ice.

"Ice? We don't have ice." So it was warm Coke and Sprite. Fortunately, the clerk took our Qatar riyals, as he couldn't make change for our US money which was denominated in twenty and hundred dollar bills.

After rejoining our group, we waited again for another hour until we were escorted to meet some hastily arranged vans. Just as we were about to leave the airport terminal, an airline employee asked to see our passports, which he took and kept.

I responded, "You can't do that. We need our passports." But he insisted that it was OK. We wouldn't be allowed to leave the terminal if we didn't leave our passports.

"What about the hotel," I protested, "They always need a passport at a hotel." He said they had made arrangements for that, and it wouldn't be a problem.

We crammed into the vans with an experienced local driver. The drive was reminiscent of our time in China; no lanes, horns honking, high speeds, near collisions, pushing others out of the way, scattering pedestrians. It was a colourful ride with lots of brightly painted buses on the road and lots of street kids trying to beg money from the foreigners. Now that we were outside the airport, we were getting a feel for the real Karachi first-hand.

After the half-hour-plus drive, we got to the gates of the Sheraton Karachi Hotel. We were not sure if this was one of the hotels that had been bombed in the past, but they behaved as if they were about to be bombed at any moment. There were heavily armed guards and armoured vehicles next to concrete and steel barriers that prevented any unwanted entry. After thorough scrutiny of our van and the passengers, the guards raised the heavy metal barricades and let us through. We had to go through another airport-like screening process at the entrance to the hotel. Once inside, life changed for the better. We were now welcomed guests, not unwelcome hostages; we were treated royally.

After some fancy, assertive maneuvers by Rochelle, we were the first ones to be served at the hotel reception. What was their first request? "Passports, please." Once we had given our frantic explanation of the absence of passports and the receptionist made a few confused phone calls, we were registered, but we had no idea for how long. We were just glad to have a luxury private room with a shower and a bed.

We were given a wonderful buffet lunch, but Pakistani food, as it turns out, is not really our favourite. It is very similar to Indian food but bland with no choice on the level spiciness.

Then we were able to finally shower and have a long-awaited nap. It was now close to 3:00 p.m. Karachi time, about fifteen hours since we left Doha. A couple hours later, we were ready to see Karachi, but was it safe?

Rochelle needed some hairspray and there was none in the hotel gift shop, so she asked the concierge where to go to get some. He volunteered to go out and buy it for her, but Rochelle wanted to get out and see what the city was like. He countered, not wanting us to venture out on our own with a suggestion that he would walk us to the store across the street. Across the street? With that crazy traffic?

He said, "No problem," and guided us through the chaotic mass of vehicles. We entered a small pharmacy/gift shop that had everything but hairspray, so we weaved our way back to the hotel, constantly being harassed by eight-to-ten-year-old professional hucksters, begging for money from the wealthy foreigners. We maneuvered our way through the hotel security without the sought-after hairspray. Again, the concierge offered to go out and find some hairspray for Rochelle.

"Normal or extra strength?" he asked. We gave him a twenty dollar bill (US funds, of course), and he was back in twenty minutes with extra strength hairspray. We didn't ask for our change, neither did he offer. The twenty-dollar can of hairspray was worth the experience, and the change from the purchase probably fed the fellow's family for the week.

While awaiting the return of our concierge, we

wandered through the hotel shops and found the prices more than reasonable for a five-star hotel; dickering was encouraged. So we bought a couple items to remind us of our experience. To this day, I still wear the reversible snakeskin belt I bought for pennies.

There was still no word on when we would leave the hotel, but we were given another buffet meal. A rumour circulated that we would still get out that night, but no one had confirmation. After the meal, we sat in our room deciding whether or not to go to bed when a note appeared under our door informing us that we needed to check out in about an hour for a 10:00 p.m. departure to the airport and a midnight departure for Kuala Lumpur and Phuket. It had now been almost twenty-four hours since we left Doha.

We were treated to another hair-raising van ride to the airport in the Karachi darkness. The vehicle was packed, but at least it was air conditioned.

Chaos reigned again at the airport as we tried to find out where to go with no passports to prove we belonged. Finally, a Qatar Airways employee showed up with a few green garbage bags filled with the three hundred passports, and no plan for how to distribute them. Again, Rochelle's assertive approach allowed us to be among the first to retrieve our passports amid the chaos.

Once finished with passport retrieval, we faced another two rounds of security screening. We were shown to our gate to await departure—it was now 10:30 p.m. local time, supposedly sixty minutes to boarding.

The next challenge was to get our boarding passes back from the same efficient employees who guided us through the passport process. Again, Rochelle provided the blocking necessary to be among the first to snatch our boarding passes from the mass of white chits sitting on the desk at the gate. The midnight departure became the 1:30 a.m. departure, but we were finally on our way to Phuket—a full day late. On to the beach.

No one ever told us the reason for the delay. We had been informed about a technical difficulty; we were later told it was a security breech. The one thing no one ever mentioned was that May 1 was the date of the raid in Abbottabad, Pakistan, when Osama Bin Laden was killed—connection? Who knows? We'll likely never find out.

The following newspaper article appeared shortly after our stop in Karachi. As if we didn't have enough to make us nervous.

***

http://www.huffingtonpost.com/2011/0
5/16/pakistan-saudi-consulate-
driver-killed_n_862275.html

Gunmen Kill Saudi Consulate Driver In Pakistan

MOHAMMAD FAROOQ and ASHRAF KHAN
05/16/11 08:12 AM ET

KARACHI, Pakistan — Gunmen on a motorbike shot and killed a Saudi diplomat as he was driving in Pakistan's largest city on Monday, just days after two hand grenades were tossed at the Arab state's consulate building, police in Karachi said.

The police believe the primary motive was sectarian tension between Islam's Sunni and Shiite branches. But the attack also follows the killing of Saudi-born Osama bin Laden in an American raid on May 2.

Al-Qaida is a fierce opponent of the Saudi regime and has sworn revenge for the death of bin Laden. But no one immediately claimed responsibility for the diplomat's slaying.

A spokesman for the Pakistani Taliban, the country's most high profile militant group, called The Associated Press to say it did not kill the diplomat.

The spokesman, Ahsanullah Ahsan, added: "Although we believe Saudi Arabia is an even bigger slave to America than Pakistan, we are not involved in today's killing."

Tariq Dharejo, a police investigator in Karachi, said officers believe the shooting was motivated by anger over Saudi Arabia's decision to send troops to Bahrain to quell protests by Shiites, who comprise 70 percent of the population there but are excluded from key positions in the Sunni-dominated government. Saudi Arabia is almost entirely Sunni.

Sunni-Shiite tensions trace back to a seventh century dispute over the true heir to Islam's Prophet Muhammad.

Monday's attack took place not far from the consulate building. The diplomat – who was driving a silver Toyota Corona and was alone – appeared to be on his way to work, said police officer Zameer Husain Abbasi. He said a 9 mm pistol was used in the assault.

The victim, identified as Hasan Khattani, was a member of the security staff at the consulate, said Iqbal Mehmood, Karachi's deputy inspector of police. He said the shooting was carried out by two men on a motorbike and appeared to be linked to last week's grenade attack on the mission, which caused some damage but no injuries.

The Saudi Foreign Ministry condemned the diplomat's killing and said in a statement issued Monday that Saudi Arabia has asked Pakistani authorities to increase security measures around the Saudi embassy and consulate in Pakistan. Prince Saudi al-Faisal, the statement said, gave condolences to the family of the slain diplomat.

Officials at the Saudi mission were not immediately available for comment.

In a statement, Pakistani Prime Minister Yousuf Raza Gilani condemned the attack and "expressed deep grief and sorrow over the tragic death of the Saudi diplomat."

Pakistan's alliance with Sunni rulers in the Middle East has come under the spotlight since the uprisings there this year. A company with strong links to the country's army announced it was sending 1,000 Pakistanis to Bahrain to help its security forces put down the Shiite uprising.

Karachi is a violent southern city of 18 million people that has been a cauldron of ethnic, sectarian and political tensions.

Saudi Arabia has funded hardline Sunnis, Iran has channeled money to Shiite groups, and in the 1980s and 1990s the country was the scene of an effective proxy war between Iran and Saudi Arabia, with Karachi an especially bloody battleground.

Several of Pakistan's Sunni extremist groups also are allied with al-Qaida and the Taliban, who view Shiites as infidels.

Saudi Arabia stripped bin Laden of citizenship and has fought al-Qaida. But money from some of its citizens is believed to help bankroll the terrorist network, which has carried out scores of attacks inside Pakistan over the last 10 years.

———

Khan reported from Islamabad.

***

The following incident occurred shortly after our "visit" to Karachi. I'm sure this hotel is not as well-guarded as our Sheraton, but again it highlights the dangers lurking in Karachi.

```
http://archive.indianexpress.com/new
s/20-injured-in-grenade-attack-at-
karachi-hotel/799318/
```

20 injured in grenade attack at Karachi hotel

Agencies Posted online: Sat Jun 04 2011, 08:47 hrs
Karachi : At least 20 people were injured today after unidentified miscreants lobbed hand grenades at a hotel in this southern port city, police said.

At least four men came to the hotel on the busy Napier road and threw grenades causing explosions and damage to the building, leaving around 20 people injured who were rushed to different hospitals for treatment, they said.

"The condition of three of the injured is precarious," a police official said.

The explosion in the hotel also damaged a gas pipeline and panic spread in the area when gas and smoke started leaking out profusely.

"The incident took place around midnight at the hotel on Thakkar road which is frequented by people till late in the night. Police and rangers personnel reached the spot and were cordoning off the affected area," he said.

According to some media reports, the hotel also doubles as a gambling den.

In the last two months, there have been two attacks on illegal gambling dens in the old areas of the city with the last one occurring on May 7 when two men lobbed grenades in Chakiwari area killing three people and injuring 21.

Earlier in April in another attack on a Rummy club in the Ghas Mandi area of Lyari, 18 people were killed and 35 injured. "We suspect these attacks to be part of an ongoing gang warfare in the old areas," the police official said.

$$\star \star \star$$

And if you're not convinced…

Here is a more recent article, long after our trip to Karachi, but it certainly highlights the danger of being in Karachi—even at the airport.

http://www.cnn.com/2014/06/08/world/asia/pakistan-karachi-airport-attack/index.html?iref=allsearch

Militants attack Karachi airport; 21 killed in clashes

From Sophia Saifi , Sanjay Gupta and Saima Mohsin , CNN
updated 12:35 AM EDT, Mon June 9, 2014
CNN.com

Karachi, Pakistan (CNN) -- Clashes at Pakistan's largest and busiest airport left more than 20 people dead after militants armed with grenades stormed into a cargo area Sunday.
Violence erupted at Jinnah International

Airport in Karachi around 11:30 p.m. Sunday and raged on for more than five hours as security forces fought off attackers, leaving some passengers trapped inside the airport.

Officials at Jinnah Hospital said the dead included eight members of airport security forces, two Pakistan International Airlines employees and one ranger.

All ten militants involved in the attack were killed, military spokesman Maj. Gen. Asim Bajwa said. Two of them detonated suicide vests, he said.

The attack ended Monday morning, and the airport is under military control, he said. It was not immediately clear who the militants were or why they staged the assault. Clashes broke out after attackers armed with grenades stormed the airport through three entrances, said Ahmad Chinoy, director-general of the citizen's police liaison committee.

One militant blew himself up in front of an armored car, leaving some people inside the vehicle critically injured, Chinoy said. A plume of smoke rose over the airport as fires raged in at least two locations. Dozens of ambulances were lined up as police and military troops swarmed the area.

A building caught fire in the attack, but no planes were damaged, Bajwa said.

The airport's cargo area is about a kilometer (0.62 miles) away from the area where commercial planes take off. Bajwa said the militants were contained in a maintenance area of the airport. "All passengers in planes evacuated to safer places," he said in a Twitter post during the clashes.

"Hunt for terrorists on."

Hours later, officials said the attack had ended and the airport was under the military's control. All flights at the airport were canceled as the violence unfolded.

In a Twitter post, Bajwa said the airport would be cleared to resume operations by midday.

Several days ago, Pakistan's government had warned provincial officials of a possible "high-profile attack on a sensitive or key installation," but the warning did not mention the airport, said Qaim Ali Shah, chief minister of Sindh province.

Earlier Sunday, at least 22 people were killed in twin suicide bomb attacks in Taftan, Pakistan, near the country's border with Iran.

Quetta Police Commissioner Qambar Dashti said no one had claimed responsibility for those attacks, which hit a hotel housing Shia pilgrims.

Pakistan Taliban 'master bomber' gunned down amid deadly infighting

* * *

Balcony Balancing Act

written by Rochelle

(Relaxing after our Karachi ordeal—May 2011)

Sitting on your balcony can even be an adventure.

After a full day of beach, coffee shops, massages, good food, and lots of walking, we returned to our Patong hotel room around 10:00 p.m. I slipped into a comfortable-but-revealing outfit and sat on our dark, secluded third-floor balcony to relax before bedtime. Brian was just getting ready for bed and was about to join me for some quiet time overlooking the picturesque pool area.

While sitting, I heard some clunking noises from behind, possibly at the next balcony; then I heard a voice, "One more floor to go." I quickly adjusted my outfit for modesty and looked over to see a young fellow on the next balcony. We were sure the room next to ours was empty, so this was quite a surprise.

After a brief hello, he drunkenly told me he was locked out of his room on the fourth floor and was climbing the balconies to get to his room. By this time, Brian had joined me and we both tried to get him to sit quietly until we got him safely out of this precarious situation. A fall from the third floor to the deck below would certainly not be good. After surviving Karachi, it would be ironic to deal with death or injury while in paradise.

The young fellow stood on the railing and reached up to the balcony above, and then he fell. Fortunately, he fell into the balcony and to safety, rather than away from it and to his death. The only mishap was when he hit his head on the balcony door. He got up, apparently unharmed due to his inebriated condition.

We decided to engage him in some light conversation to try to get him to forget his climbing objective. We found out he was a young American military guy from Tucson, Arizona, and was on leave. We convinced him to sit tight while Brian went to call security to let the fellow into the next room and out of this predicament.

While we continued our conversation with the young, polite-but-very-drunk soldier, a couple of staff appeared at the pool area below and the security guard started shouting from below. They fired off a couple of dumb-ass questions and comments like, "What are you doing there? Get down."

Brian shouted back at them to just go and get a key to the next room and let him in. I went out into the hall while Brian tried to keep the young man from doing anything stupid. Finally, a staff member wandered down the hall, and I and shouted to him to open the hotel room next to us. Reluctantly, he complied and brought the young drunk through the room and into the hall.

The soldier thanked me profusely and gave me a big hug.

End of the evening? Almost.

Shortly after, while we continued relaxing, our buddy appeared on his balcony above us and started to shout down telling us what a great couple we were, we deserved the world, and he owed us big. Brian told him that our reward was seeing him safe. He finally bid us an emotional good night, and our adventure was finally over.

When we saw him the next morning, he displayed no sign of recognizing us as his hotel neighbours or saviours and likely had little recollection of his near-death experience.

Mediterranean Madness
October 2008

"I'm in big trouble."

Those are not the words you want to hear from your wife just hours before her return from a solo vacation. The thoughts that go through your mind in the instant before you uncover the facts behind the ominous message—Sickness? Injury? Death? In fact, other than these three fears, Rochelle delivered what is the worst possible news while travelling.

"My passport has been stolen." She shivered the words through the invisible lines connecting our mobile phones—hers in Cyprus, mine in the United Arab Emirates. I could tell by her voice that she was in a state of emotional shock.

Rochelle's revelation was preceded by my phone ringing with the caller ID indicating Rochelle's phone, but it wasn't Rochelle's voice that responded to my hi there. It was our friend Ada, who coincidently was vacationing on her own in Cyprus where the two ladies had crossed paths.

"Hi, Brian. This is Ada. Rochelle needs to speak to you," Ada announced and passed the phone to Rochelle who issued her devastating words.

Living in a Muslim country, we were subject to the various customs and rituals of the local population. Having just returned from our summer vacation at the end of August 2008, we were faced with the first month of teaching at our college during the holy month of Ramadan. Ramadan ended on

September 29, which signalled the start of Eid al-Fitr—a national holiday with a week off work. Our summer vacation was still a vivid, recent memory, and I was not ready to take a travel holiday so soon. I just wanted to take advantage of the cooling desert weather to work on my training for the upcoming triathlon season. But Rochelle was eager to take a vacation, so I urged her to take a solo trip to Cyprus and do some touring for a few days. Cyprus was the nearest non-Muslim country and travelling in a Muslim country during Eid can be a challenge.

Rochelle arrived in Larnaca, Cyprus, on Monday, September 29, 2008, with an expected return date of Thursday, October 2. She stayed in a hotel a short bus ride away from airport and enjoyed taking various organized tours around the Greek section of the island of Cyprus. During her travels she met up with Ada who worked at our college and was also travelling solo. They kept each other company on much of the trip.

Rochelle had the first couple of rainy days to herself but was enjoying the experience as seen in her initial email:

Hi there

Well I am here, safe and sound.

One problem!

The weather!

It's pouring rain. *No one on the beaches! No one around the pool!*

No one sitting out at all the sidewalk cafés.

It hasn't rained in over a year so the locals are all happy, but the tourists (me) are finding it a bit annoying.

Oh well if you can't sit on the beach—go exploring! Go shopping!

Partly to save money, but mainly to get into the spirit of exploring the local environment, I decided to take the local bus into downtown Larnaca. So there I stood, out in the rain with a bunch of people who looked as if they were going in to work. After about twenty minutes, the bus came along and, of course, by then we were all drenched.

The bus trip was about ten minutes to the middle of the town. I had fun wandering around even though it was raining. I found a bookstore. I found a shoe store. And finally I found an Internet bar so I could send this message.

For tomorrow, I have booked a trip to Nicosia, the Troodos Mountains, and a traditional village called Omodos. The next day it's Famagusta.

I have taken some pictures of me sitting all alone in an outdoor café by the empty beach, and I even asked one of the people waiting for the bus with me to take a picture of me waiting in the rain.

More to follow tomorrow after I get back from the tour. Hopefully, the weather cooperates.

Love,

Rochelle

At the end of the trip, Rochelle and Ada packed up and met for a bus ride to the airport, as they were departing on the same plane from the Larnaca airport. Along the way to the airport, they stopped at a tourist shop to pick up some last-minute souvenirs to take home. In the bus to the airport,

Rochelle discovered the source of the two-week nightmare that was about to unfold.

When she reached into her purse to produce her passport, she found the slot containing her wallet which housed all of her required travel items—passport, credit cards, cash, itinerary—was missing. Her only explanation was that it must have been removed from her purse at the souvenir shop. The only things of value remaining in her purse were here mobile phone and her Palm Pilot PDA. These two items were the only things separating her from complete obliteration from the human race. Without a passport in a foreign country, you are nobody—on par with street scum. No one wants to help you; no one cares. With her two devices of communication, she at least had a link to a world that knew she existed.

Rochelle had begged the airline agent to let

her board the plane. After all, her name was on the list. But the agent said she was not allowed to board anyone without a passport. Besides, if she did, Rochelle would just be arrested at her destination for travelling without documentation.

After pumping as much information as I could from Rochelle, who was barely coherent in her description of events, I asked to speak to Ada. Ada was a seasoned traveller and might have some ideas on how to move forward from this point.

Ada had already thought through some of the immediate issues. They had gone to the police station to file a report of the theft, and they had called the Canadian Consulate in Nicosia. First, Rochelle would need to get to the Canadian Consulate, about a forty-minute bus ride from Larnaca. However, it was Thursday and they were closing, so Rochelle could only make that trip on Friday morning. Second, Rochelle needed cash. Ada left Rochelle what little cash she had, which amounted to under a hundred euros. I would have to send Rochelle some cash using Western Union. Ada even knew of the nearest Western Union agent in Larnaca.

Ada was very helpful and sympathetic, but there was little more she could do and her plane was already boarding. She offered to stay with Rochelle. As much as I wished she could stay and keep Rochelle company during the ordeal, I could tell that Ada was not enthused with her offer. I told her to just board her plane, and I would deal with the situation. Ada departed, leaving Rochelle in tears at the airport not really knowing what to do next. Rochelle had never used the texting feature of her phone before, but it became her lifeline as we communicated continually by text. Ada had given her a few pointers on texting.

The two tasks planned for Friday were trying to get Rochelle some cash and having Rochelle go to the Canadian Consulate in Nicosia. However, Friday's chores were irrelevant if she didn't get through Thursday night. How can you do that in a foreign country with no credit cards, no ID, and almost no cash? I could feel her anguish through the pained texts that appeared regularly on my phone, and there was nothing I could do to help, causing me an almost equal agony.

Rochelle found an Internet café where she was able to do some email work and make an online booking with Expedia.com. I immediately cancelled her credit cards with the bank, but she had photos of my credit cards on her Palm Pilot. She was able to book the Sun Hall Hotel in Larnaca for Friday, Saturday, and Sunday nights with the hope that she would have everything sorted out for a Monday departure. Very wishful thinking as will be seen. She made sure that meals were included in the booking in case she still didn't have cash. Expedia will not let you book a hotel for the same day, so although the next three days were taken care of she still had no place to stay on Thursday night.

With her hotel booking printout from the Internet café, Rochelle trudged over to the Sun Hall Hotel to see if she could arrange a room for the night. She showed them the booking for the next day, but that didn't help for Thursday night. With some begging, pleading, and a few tears, she was able to get the desk clerk to take pity on her. He offered a room for the night.

Then came the issue of registering without any identification. It turns out that photocopies of ID or pictures on your PDA, although they make you feel secure, are absolutely useless accessories. People want to see the originals. Also, hotel check-in procedures around the world call for an imprint of a credit card to register. A few more tears convinced the desk clerk to check her in with the ID from the Palm Pilot and secured her room for the night and the following three nights. But she had to use up much of her precious cash to pay for the Thursday night stay.

Early morning texts told me of a sleepless night in Larnaca with lots of tossing, turning, and lonely tears. Friday in the city of Al Ain where we lived is called yawm-al-jum'ah or prayer day or mosque day. It is equivalent to Sunday church in the Christian world. In addition, we were still in the midst of Eid al-Fitr, the holiday. I knew I could get cash from an ATM, but I wasn't sure when or if I could wire it to Rochelle in Larnaca. Although the malls would likely open at 10:00 a.m., most retailers would not open until at least 2:00 p.m. or even 4:00 p.m. I needed the services of our money transfer kiosk, and I didn't know if it would be open.

With my five thousand UAE dirhams from the ATM, I went to the mall at opening time to see if I could send the money. However, Rochelle's main Friday task was to get to Nicosia to start the process of replacing her stolen passport, so the cash transfer would need to wait a day. With Rochelle's busy Friday schedule and the Friday closures in Al Ain, I was only able to get the money to Rochelle on Saturday morning.

As first in line, I was able to use their Western Union service to send money to Rochelle in Larnaca. All Rochelle had to do was show up at the Western Union outlet in Larnaca, which was walking distance from her hotel, provide them with the access code I was given and a piece of ID. There we go again. How you produce ID that was stolen?

Rochelle was able to convince the Larnaca agent to accept her ID on the Palm Pilot, but only after I talked to the agent on the phone.

So now Rochelle had enough cash to keep her going but no hope of anything happening until Monday. One of her sources of connection to the outside world was through the Internet using a nearby Internet café. She used this to send emails and to post to our blog site.

Here is Rochelle's initial post to our website:

Still in Cyprus
by Rochelle

Introduction: I want to go home!

Yes, I am still in Cyprus!

Are you ready for the story?

A couple of hours before I was to fly home, I was out

doing some last-minute shopping with one our fellow teachers from Al Ain who happened to be travelling in Cyprus as well.

We stopped to have a bite to eat before taking the bus to the airport. On the bus, I looked in my purse—and my whole wallet was gone! Everything including my passport, credit cards, driver's license, etc.

We immediately went to the police to report it and then headed to the airport with the police report. But I was going nowhere without a passport.

So, from the airport I called the Canadian Consulate in Nicosia. Very matter of fact, they told me I must come to them and apply for a new passport. I could only come on Friday because they closed at noon. I tried to explain my situation, but they just kept repeating you cannot travel without the proper identification. Even if the airline were to let me on the plane, the destination country would not let me in.

I called Brian to break the news to him. He was sick, but there was little he could do. He faxed me photocopies of my ID, but they did not help me to get on the plane.

My friend gave me all the cash she had, and the plane took off without me.

I was stuck in Larnaca with no identification and only one hundred and fifty euros. I gathered up all the UAE dirhams I had put away for when I got home and exchanged them for euros. I then had about four hundred euros.

I talked to Brian, and I found I had his credit card information on my Palm Pilot. He suggested I go to an Internet bar and book a room online.

It worked!

Only problem, it was already after 5:00 p.m., and I couldn't book a room for Thursday night.

I went to the hotel I had booked for the next day and showed them my confirmation and told them my sad story. I asked them, "Please, I need a room tonight."

Luckily, they had a room that included supper and breakfast so at least I had a bed and food. But I had to use eighty-five of my euros.

After a sleepless night, I was up the next morning (Friday) and on the bus to Nicosia. I was at the office when it opened and I filled out forms, ran around getting photos, and went to a bank to get a money order to Canada for two hundred twenty Canadian dollars. Now I was down to sixty euros.

The whole ordeal in the office was not a positive experience. I had no idea how long the process would take and got no answers other than it takes time and to be patient.

The forms I filled out Friday had to go to Damascus, the nearest Canadian Embassy. They hoped they would get away Friday, and they hoped the Embassy could start looking at it on Monday!

Meanwhile, Brian had to make a trip into the Canadian Embassy on Sunday to give them my birth certificate so they could fax it to Damascus.

I needed to get references in Canada that Canadian officials could phone to identify me.

So, it is now Saturday. Here I am in Larnaca.

Maybe something will happen on Monday, but I doubt it. I don't think I am going anywhere until near the end of the week if I am lucky.

And back to the money issue.

With no ID, wiring money through the Western Union was a bit tricky but with the photocopies of my IDs Brian had emailed me, Brian was able to wire me money, and I was able to pick it up.

So I have cash, a hotel, and food.

Brian and the people back in Al Ain are being great, but there is very little they can do. My mobile works here so Brian and I are in constant contact with text messages or calling.

But *when will I get home? It's still up in the air.*

This story isn't over yet.

I will keep you up to date. Care packages to Larnaca, Cyprus, would be greatly appreciated.

R

The Canadian Consulate in Nicosia, almost an hour's bus ride from Larnaca, is not a true full-functioning consulate. It is what is called an honourary consulate and is only open from 9:00 a.m. to noon Monday to Friday. None of the staff is even Canadian but, rather, poorly trained locals who enjoy working half days and not having much to do. They were not thrilled to see Rochelle enter with her problem. It turns out they could do little more than gather paper and send it to the full-functioning consulate in nearby Damascus, Syria. Syria, being a

Muslim country, and one that had not yet changed its weekend as some of its Arabian Gulf compatriots (it used to be Thursday and Friday but is now Friday and Saturday), was closed on Friday for yawm-al-jum'ah, or prayer day. They would open on Saturday after their Thursday and Friday weekend.

The less-than-helpful consulate worker, obviously conscious of the clock ticking toward her weekend, listened and took notes as Rochelle related her story of woe. She listed the things that Rochelle would need to process her papers and hopefully get a travel document needed to escape her paradise prison.

First on the to-do list was to fill out the appropriate forms, which the consulate had on hand. Rochelle would need two passport photos, and, fortunately, there was a photographer nearby that Rochelle could use. She would need a guarantor to attest to Rochelle being who she said she was. This, of course, would be a major problem as Rochelle knew no one in this strange land, let alone anyone who knew her for the required two years. The attendant came to Rochelle's rescue on this matter, informing her that the manager of the consulate was licensed to attest to a swearing of identity. Rochelle needed to provide the police report that she had in hand. Also she needed to provide the names of two people in Canada whom the passport office could call to confirm her identity. I made sure we had two people sitting by the phone to await the calls. Money, of course, was necessary for processing the documents, thus Rochelle's need to get a money order from the bank, depleting her precious cash supply. The final item was for Rochelle to provide a government-issued identification such as a birth certificate. Rochelle's birth certificate was not among the items stolen as it was in the dresser drawer next to our bed in Al Ain. One of the few pieces of good luck during this time in purgatory.

Rochelle called me to see if I could find the birth certificate, which was easy to locate but difficult to transmit to Nicosia. They would not accept a fax or scanned copy from me; it had to be the original or a fax from the Canadian Consulate in the UAE once they had certified it was real. Sending the original by mail or courier did not seem to be the wisest move, so I elected to use the consulate in Abu Dhabi. This, of course, was the weekend in the UAE—Friday and Saturday. I would not be able to get to the consulate in Abu Dhabi, a ninety-minute drive from our city of Al Ain, until Sunday morning, when I was supposed return to work after the Eid holiday. This meant that the honourary consulate in Nicosia would not be able to process it until Monday, after their weekend. But that would have to do.

Rochelle had been victimized by theft and, as often happens, victims start to blame themselves for their predicament. Rochelle was no different as seen in this email she sent to me during the ordeal.

Rochelle's email, October 3, 2008:

What a Mess
Just talked to you. I really needed that right now.
I feel pretty upset with myself.

I feel embarrassed to come back home after being so stupid.

How do I get through the next few days just waiting around? And will Damascus not want more stuff?

When she asked how my name is Bos, I told her I had my name changed legally. She had me write that out on a paper. In Canada, I think we had to send in the documents.

I am sure we had to send a lot of other stuff, but all I can do is sit here and wait.

As I told you on the phone, the hotel has told me I have breakfast and dinner included in my room.

I think they are doing it to be nice, but at least I have food and a bed.

Will I ever get home?

Love,

R

I know that we weren't the first travellers to ever experience a lost passport, so I decided to call the Canadian government emergency number for lost or stolen passports. This proved to be a useless exercise as all they really wanted was the report of the stolen document which Rochelle had already done through the consulate in Nicosia. They could or would do nothing more. They offered to provide cash on loan, but that was not one of our issues. All they did was reinforce that Rochelle had to deal with the consulate in Nicosia who in turn would communicate with Damascus who would do whatever was necessary with Ottawa while Abu Dhabi would have to play their role. Quite the daisy chain.

Rochelle quickly got her passport photos taken and got the attestation done by the consulate manager before the Friday noon closure. It would be Monday before they had all the documents they needed to send to the real consulate in Damascus for processing. Rochelle had from Friday noon until Monday morning to fret over her predicament. There was nothing more she could do—her fate was in the hands of the consulate in Nicosia, the consulate in Damascus, the consulate in Abu Dhabi, and me. All she could do was sit and cry, which she did—lots.

Both Rochelle and I were using prepaid phones with the credits rapidly eroding. I was able to continuously replenish our prepaid accounts from Al Ain, otherwise Rochelle's only lifeline would disintegrate.

With lots of texting and phone calls, we got through the weekend. For me, my weekend concluded on Sunday morning when I drove into Abu Dhabi with Rochelle's birth certificate. I was fortunate to have no classes to teach in the morning so I was able to arrive at the consulate at opening time and get attended to immediately. They took a photocopy of the birth certificate and assured me they would fax it to Nicosia immediately, but I would not be able to get confirmation of receipt until the next day, Monday, when the Cyprus consulate would open.

Rochelle made lots of trips to the Internet café. Here is a post to our website from Sunday, October 4:

Going nowhere yet

by Rochelle

Introduction: Still here!

My application for a temporary passport has moved from Nicosia (Friday) to Damascus (Sunday) to Canada today (Monday).

I talked to Canada as soon as the passport office was opened this morning and got very little satisfaction. They told me the embassy in Damascus will get in touch with me when they are finished looking at my application. I tried to explain my situation, so she checked to see if my file was in the system yet. It wasn't! So she told me to call back later in the day. I will!

Sent an emergency email to the Canadian passport office and got an email back telling me to get in touch with the offices in Nicosia. Thanks a lot.

A game of waiting that I am not good at.

If I sound a bit frustrated that is an understatement!

R

Monday morning, Rochelle made her second (third, if you count her holiday trip) bus ride to Nicosia to hopefully finalize everything for her travel document. She knew she only had a three-hour window from 9:00 a.m. to noon to get everything done.

It turned out that the passport photos Rochelle provided were not satisfactory, and she had to repeat the process. Now the local agent assured Rochelle that they had all the necessary documents and would forward them to Damascus for processing. That was all they could do for today, and it would be Tuesday before Damascus could start to process the documents. Rochelle returned to Larnaca to sit and stew until the next day when she would repeat the trip. In the meantime, I was sitting helplessly in the middle of the desert not knowing when I would see my wife again.

Tuesday, Rochelle returned by bus to the consulate in Nicosia, hoping but not expecting, her ordeal to come to a close. She even had her bag packed and ready in her hotel room, as her reservation had run out, in the event she could return to Larnaca and proceed to the airport.

Rochelle arrived at the consulate before the opening time of 9:00 a.m. and could see people moving behind the locked door. However, there was no way they were going to unlock the door before the appointed opening time or five to ten minutes after. They assured her that Damascus would have the package and they would commence processing it. Rochelle waited around Nicosia until she saw some evidence of communication between Nicosia and Damascus. Approaching noon, the dreaded closing time, she finally got word that Damascus had in fact received the documents, but they were not complete. Apparently, Abu Dhabi had only photocopied and faxed the front of Rochelle's birth certificate and not both the front and back as required.

As she was edged out of the consulate due to the noon closing time, she was able to get contact information for the consulate in Damascus and called them to find out the problem. They confirmed that they did not have enough information to send the package to Ottawa for processing. They needed to have a certified copy of the back side of the birth certificate. I received her frantic phone call and became agitated and angry. Abu Dhabi was a ninety-minute drive away, and I likely couldn't make it before the consulate closed. I had done everything right—it was the consulate people in Abu Dhabi that screwed up, but Rochelle was paying the price for their mistake.

I called the consulate in Damascus who insisted they have the back side of the birth certificate and that they required the original or a fax from the Abu Dhabi consulate. There was no give and limited sympathy for our predicament.

I was able to get in touch with a clerk at the Abu Dhabi consulate who put me in touch with the person who had served me when I brought the birth certificate two days earlier. She apologized and agreed it was her fault, not mine, but that didn't solve our problem. With a final act of compassion, she offered to allow me to scan and email the back of the birth certificate to her. She would then print it off and fax it to Damascus as if she had done it from the original. She rationalized that she had already seen the original, so it should be OK. I did my part and she did hers. By the end of the business day on Tuesday, Damascus had all the material they needed to process the documents starting the next day, Wednesday.

Rochelle's next website post:

Six days and still waiting to go home

by Rochelle

Introduction: I've been here six days since I was supposed to fly back to Dubai.

Wednesday

Tomorrow will be a week since I was supposed to fly back home.

Some progress, followed by two steps back.

Yesterday I was told that they had started the process of issuing me a new passport. Good news. *When will that process be done? No one will give me a straight answer.*

Today I talked to the embassy in Nicosia to see where things were at. Big problem. *When Brian went to Abu Dhabi to give them my birth certificate to be sent to the consulate in Damascus, they only sent one side of the certificate, not the back side. The process of issuing me a new passport cannot continue or be finished until they get that.*

On the phone to Brian. He calls Abu Dhabi. Yes, they had made a mistake and only sent the front. Luckily, they let him just email them both sides (instead of another two-hour drive into Abu Dhabi), and they now have sent that on to the embassy in Damascus.

I have now talked to the embassies in Damascus and in Nicosia and supposedly the process is back on track.

Hopefully, no new problems.

Good news.

Brian is flying in tomorrow for the weekend.

I am sure he would rather kill me, but instead he is flying to see me.

We will try to make the best of it and have a nice weekend here in Cyprus.

Love from Cyprus

Maybe I might even be able to fly home with him, but we are not counting on it.

Rochelle made her daily journey from Larnaca to Nicosia on Wednesday with little expectation that she would be any further ahead at the end of this visit. She was right. By the time the noon closing time arrived in Nicosia, there was no word of completion from Damascus. If the travel document was not in the Nicosia Consulate when she arrived Thursday morning, she would lose another weekend. The Damascus weekend started at the end of business on Wednesday, and they wouldn't open until Saturday morning. Nicosia would be closed by then for their weekend and wouldn't open until Monday morning. It was clear that Rochelle needed to make another trip to the Internet café to book more time in her hotel. They were still not prepared to extend her stay at the desk as she didn't have a credit card to secure the room.

Rochelle was confined to her hotel room for much of her solo stay. The consulate in Nicosia was not prepared to incur international long distance charges by calling her mobile phone which used a UAE country code. They insisted on using her hotel room phone as the contact number. This meant that during the limited hours the consulate was open in Nicosia, she had to sit in her room waiting for a call that never came. She occupied herself by watching the sole English-speaking TV station that seemed to only show reruns of David Hasselhoff in *Knight Rider* talking to his supercar KITT.

With both of us in a state of despair and resigned to at least three more days of captivity, I elected to ask for some compassionate time off work and fly to Cyprus to spend the weekend with Rochelle. I wasn't sure Rochelle's emotional state would allow her to survive another weekend on her own. I wasn't sure I could either.

I arrived in Larnaca on Thursday with Rochelle meeting me at the airport. There was still a slim chance that if Damascus had processed the paperwork Rochelle could get her travel document on Thursday or Friday and perhaps even accompany me home. Well, it was a hope anyway. A quick call to the Nicosia Consulate confirmed that they had received nothing yet from Damascus and, of course, they would be closing at noon, but we could check back on Friday. We knew if there was nothing in the Friday morning mail at the Nicosia consulate that nothing more would happen until at least Monday. With the Damascus weekend being Thursday and Friday, the only way Nicosia could receive any documents on Friday was if Damascus had processed and sent them on Wednesday before their office closed for the weekend.

So Rochelle and I tried to make the most of our romantic weekend in Cyprus. In spite of the tension from the circumstances, we really enjoyed each other's company. Rochelle was relieved to have some support at her side. She was a wreck from all the events. At least I had my credit cards and ID, so I could secure the hotel room for the next couple of nights without the hassle of using the Internet café and begging the hotel clerks.

It was a sad goodbye when I left Larnaca on Saturday evening. Rochelle would have at least another full day on her own before finding out on Monday whether or not she would be able to leave. To continue the misfortune from this ill-fated excursion that started almost two weeks earlier, I encountered a five-hour delay in Manama, Bahrain, where my connection was to take me to Dubai, and I arrived back home in Al Ain just in time to have a quick shower and get to work for Sunday morning classes.

I posted about the Cyprus trip on our website:

From Cyprus

I arrived here Thursday p.m. Rochelle is still pretty upset. Apparently, Syria has now finally processed the travel documents. They sent them out Thursday, but did not arrive in Nicosia on Friday. So another weekend goes by.

Hopefully, Rochelle can pick everything up on Monday a.m. and be on her way home that day.

I leave today (Saturday). Rochelle is not happy about that.

We had a nice quiet weekend in Larnaca—walking, sitting on the beach. It was helpful for Rochelle. She was able to sleep and eat with me here. Those activities were absent during the height of the crisis.

Hopefully, in a couple of days this will all be behind us and we can get back to normal—whatever that is.

My students, all female Emiratis, were concerned for me and for Rochelle, whom they knew well. Throughout the ordeal, they offered to get their fathers to help us out with their influence, or "wasta" as it is called in the Gulf countries. Many of our students were connected to the royal family or were wealthy in their own right and had grown up knowing that their powerful fathers could make things happen. What they didn't realize was that their fathers' wasta did not extend beyond the borders of the UAE. So I respectfully declined their offer.

Sunday passed with lots of texts between Larnaca and Al Ain and a couple of phone calls. There was nothing more either of us could do but wait until the Nicosia Consulate opened on Monday morning and find out if Damascus had done their job at the start of their work week, during Nicosia's weekend.

Rochelle's website post on Sunday:

Hopefully I fly home tomorrow.

Sunday

It was great having Brian here for a couple of days, and things almost seemed normal.

But yesterday he was off to Al Ain without me! Not a happy situation. And then Brian ran into problems on his flight home and was delayed in Bahrain for five hours, not arriving home until basically he only had time to shower, shave, and go to work.

Tomorrow I will be on the first bus into Nicosia and hopefully *my passport will be waiting for me. But that is not the end of the nightmare yet. I then must get back to Larnaca, get my bags, get to the airport and* hopefully *get a seat on the plane. (There is only one plane a day to Abu Dhabi at 3:40 p.m.)*

If all goes smoothly, I could be home Monday night around midnight. Keep your fingers crossed and any other parts of your body!

On Monday, Rochelle hustled to the bus station for the first departure to Nicosia, not wanting to await a phone confirmation of the arrival of her travel document. She was waiting at the front door of the consulate at opening time. They knew her well by this time and invited her to sit while they opened the morning mail delivery that had just arrived. It was there. A passport-like document with a white rather than black cover, and only a few pages. Other than that, it looked like a passport.

Rochelle was so excited. She could hardly hold the document in her hands. Her fingers trembled as she pushed the buttons on her overused phone to text me that she had the document in her hands. I texted her back to tell her to put the document in her bra or panties to keep it safe. I'm sure that unsecured papers whooshed to the floor in the consulate from the breeze that Rochelle created as she rushed back to the bus station to return to the hotel and collect her items for the short ride to the airport.

At the airport, she could have used her return ticket if she wanted to wait for the appointed departure, but she was prepared to pay any price to catch the next plane out and used her cash to secure the next available seat. She had some hassles in getting them to accept her odd-looking travel document.

Other than when she was in the air and required to turn off her phone, she was sending me constant texts informing me of her progress away from her two-week-plus prison. After her minor trouble getting out of Cyprus with her document, Rochelle was concerned with what kind of reception she would get in Abu Dhabi with the temporary passport.

Rochelle texted me upon her touchdown in Abu Dhabi, but then it was some time before I got the next communication indicating that there was some hassle at passport control with her new document and no visa in it, but they stamped her through with a visit visa, indicating she had thirty days in the country to get her paperwork sorted out. It never occurred to her to check the stamp, after all who checks the stamp on their passport.

Rochelle's last communication written Oct. 12:

Monday I was up early and on the bus to Nicosia to hopefully pick up my new passport and then get back and get a flight out of Cyprus.

Finally, good news—it was there—a temporary passport, not the real thing but a legal travel document.

I grabbed a cab back to Larnaca and went right out to the airport with all my luggage, ready to go. But I could not find anyone at the airport who would sell me a ticket. They didn't like the look of my temporary passport and told me to come back later just before the flight.

So, I got back in a cab with my luggage and went into town. I went to a travel agent and told her the story. She phoned the airport and a few other people and said I should be OK. So I now have a ticket!

Back to the airport. In line to board. They were not too happy, but with the police report and other copied documents I was allowed on.

My next hurdle was getting back into the UAE in Abu Dhabi.

Again, they were not happy with my documents and many people had to come and look at my stuff but finally they let me in!

So, I am back home.

I am told in about sixty days a proper, new passport will arrive in Abu Dhabi, but right now I will believe it when it happens. I'm just glad it is over!

It was an eternal taxi ride that brought Rochelle back to our home where she collapsed from relief. The travel ordeal was now over. But there was more yet to come.

We allowed ourselves a few days of celebration and relaxation to recover, but not long after her return, well within the promised sixty days, her permanent passport arrived at the Abu Dhabi Consulate. Rochelle drove in to pick it up, remembering to bring her temporary document with her. She signed for and received her new clean and empty passport with a disclaimer on page five that said that this document was replacing a stolen document. The clerk at the counter asked Rochelle if she want her cancelled temporary passport back or if it could be destroyed. Rochelle's first thought was to discard it with the remainder of the unpleasant memory of its origin. On second thought, however, she decided to hang onto the obsolete document just in case. That afterthought proved to be prophetic as it contained the only evidence that Rochelle had entered the country legally. The date stamp on the visit visa stamp, with a yet undiscovered date error, proved that she had not snuck into the country.

With her new passport in hand, Rochelle was able to get our visa officer, Walid, to start the process of replacing her stolen resident permit to replace her thirty-day visit visa. Thank goodness Rochelle was at home for this next long ordeal and not stuck in some foreign land.

Walid took Rochelle to the immigration office in Al Ain to get a new resident visa placed in her brand new, empty passport. Most of the officials spoke either only Arabic or barely passable English, so in addition to not knowing the process, Rochelle faced a language barrier, making Walid, a fluent English and Arabic speaker, essential to the success of this venture.

Walid explained the background of the situation to the immigration officer. When Walid handed the officer the new passport and requested a new visa, the officer said he needed to cancel the old visa.

"Where is the old visa?" he asked. Walid again explained that it was in the stolen passport. The officer said he needed the old visa to cancel it or a police report to prove its loss. Rochelle rifled through her purse and found the wrinkled and tattered document and handed it to Walid who in turn passed it to the immigration officer.

The officer examined it and turned it over several times in his hand and said, "Where is the stamp?"

"Stamp?" Rochelle asked, "What stamp?" Walid was relegated to the sidelines while an agitated Rochelle took over the discussion.

"Your police report must be stamped by the UAE Embassy in the country where the theft occurred," he replied. "You will have to go back and get the embassy to stamp it."

"You mean fly back to Cyprus and get this document stamped there?" Rochelle questioned with surprise.

The officer nodded.

"That's ridiculous," Rochelle exclaimed. "I can't go back to Cyprus. First of all, I can't even get out of the country without some kind of visa in my passport. That's why I'm here, to get a visa."

"Maybe you could get a friend to go for you, then," he said, attempting some strange form of local logic.

"Where is the embassy in Cyprus?" Walid asked, trying to reclaim some usefulness.

The officer clicked on his computer and replied, "There is no UAE Embassy in Cyprus; you need to use the embassy in Damascus."

Rochelle let out an exasperated sigh at this "Abbott and Costello" routine unfolding before her eyes.

Then, the officer asked, "Where is your entry stamp?" looking at Rochelle's empty passport.

"It's in my temporary passport," she replied, handing the white, cancelled document to the officer.

"This document is not valid. It has been voided," he commented as he looked at the white cover with the clipped corner and the "cancelled" stamp on the first page.

"They had to void it when I claimed my new passport," Rochelle explained. "I kept it because it contains my entry stamp and visit visa."

The officer thumbed through the thin document stopping at the page with the entry stamp. "Visit visas are only for thirty days; this one is expired. You have overstayed and must pay a penalty."

"What do you mean expired? I only got home within the last week," Rochelle blurted out in part angry and in part afraid.

"See," the immigration officer flipped to the page to show Rochelle the stamp. Obviously, the less-than-efficient passport control officer at the airport had not set his stamp properly, and the last number, instead of being an eight for the year 2008, was a zero, indicating the year 2000, resulting in an eight-year overstay. At one hundred United Arab Emirates dirhams per day, that amounted to almost three hundred thousand dirhams or over eighty thousand dollars in penalties.

Rochelle protested and Walid blustered, but the immigration official would not be swayed by any fact or logic at this most improbable situation. The police report needed a stamp from a non-existent embassy and the erroneous fine must be paid.

Walid muttered something to Rochelle and escorted her back to the college with vague assurances that he would do something.

It became clear over the next week that Walid did not know what to do to fix the problem and was hard to locate as he seemed to be hiding from us when we tried to get status updates.

Walid took Rochelle for a couple more visits to the immigration office, but Rochelle never could figure out what was going on with the discussions Walid conducted in Arabic. Each time, they left with nothing new having happened.

After a couple of weeks of no action, I finally walked into the campus director's office and begged with him.

"Brent," I pleaded, "I hate to bother you with this, but we can't seem to make any progress in getting this visa issue resolved. Walid can't get through to the people, and no one wants to help. I don't know where to turn."

Brent took matters into his hands, but as a Canadian, like us, he had no knowledge of how to solve the problem. He went to Walid's boss, John, who in turn approached Walid with a stern warning, "Take Rochelle down to the immigration office. Get this thing fixed and don't come back until it is done."

Walid understood the nature of the order and realized that his job might be on the line if he couldn't get this fixed. Over half of his job was securing resident visas for employees and families, and if he couldn't do that, there was little need for his function.

Walid took Rochelle back to the visa office and went from one office another with Rochelle in tow and not understanding a word of the many heated discussions that took place. Each office they entered seemed to be bigger than the previous one, and each uniformed official had more stripes and bars on his uniform than the last.

In the final office, the older official took Rochelle's passport, clicked some buttons on the computer, disappeared for a while, returned with a resident visa glued to page twenty of the passport, and did not request payment for the obviously bogus fine.

The long ordeal was finally over.

Heathrow Hell—by Rochelle
March 2008

The phone call came while I was entertaining our guests during a supper cruise on an Arabian Dhow in Dubia. Having just finished our meal, I made a necessary trip to the toilet only to be met by Rob, Lori's boyfriend, as I exited the ladies room. Little did I know that Rob had chosen that moment to ask for my daughter's hand in marriage. Before he could blurt out the never to be uttered words, my mobile phone rang.

Brian, calling from Al Ain, broke the news to me that my eighty-eight-year-old father had passed away in Regina, Canada. My son, also named Rob, had just called Brian to relay the bad news, and Brian had delayed telling me until he was reasonably certain our group had finished supper. Given there was little anyone could do, Brian didn't want to cast a dark cloud too early on the evening merriments.

Rob, Lori, and the rest of our company, who had been staying at our UAE home and enjoying the warmth of the late spring, would be leaving the next day, Friday, to return to their lives back in Canada. Brian was able to book me on the first available British Airways flight, leaving almost twelve hours before Lori's crew was to leave, allowing me to arrive in Regina long before the rest of the crowd joined me for the funeral.

In addition to having to make funeral arrangements, I was the executor of my dad's meager estate and I would have paperwork to clear up before returning to my home half a world away.

I threw together a bag of essentials when I returned to Al Ain from Dubai and was in a taxi bound for the Dubai airport shortly after midnight for a 4:00 a.m. departure through London Heathrow and on to Calgary and Regina. Our guests would be getting a good night's sleep prior to their later departure on Friday, and I planned on being in Regina long before Lori would be able to catch up with me. That plan took a wrong turn.

I caught some rest on the Dubai to London leg of the trip and wasn't expecting a long layover in London before heading on to Canada. Boy was I wrong! Long layover does not even begin to describe the hell that awaited me upon landing at London's Heathrow Airport.

My Friday, March 28, 2008, landing coincided with the long-anticipated opening of Terminal 5 at London Heathrow. On this day, British Airways experienced the largest computer failure in their history.

I arrived at Terminal 4, on time at 1:30 p.m. With only ninety minutes until my 3:00 p.m. departure from Terminal 5, I had to hustle as there are always multiple layers of security to go through in this active airport.

A quick glance at the board gave the first hint of the nightmare that I was entering. My flight had the word "cancelled" beside it. Not "on-time," "delayed," or some other such annoyance, but "cancelled" as in "not going anywhere." I was too disturbed by this news to notice the chaos emerging around me. I didn't even notice that all other flights on the departure board had the same frightening word beside them.

I rushed to the British Airways desk and was told to go to the departure area to rebook my flight. Once arriving at the departure area, the real horror of my situation began to register. I joined a horrendous lineup filled with confused, tired, and angry travellers.

One hour had passed since my landing, putting me in the chaotic lineup at 2:30 p.m. where I stood for five hours until I finally got to the front of the line to receive my rebooking through Frankfurt on Lufthansa. Unlike many of the stranded passengers, the airline gave me a hotel and food voucher to hold me over until the flight took off the next morning.

In my hotel room, the first thing on my mind was to call Brian and let him know what was happening. I called from the room and started to feel maybe things would be OK. I would just be a day late getting home. Our company had not even left Al Ain yet, so I thought I could still beat everyone to the funeral. Wrong again.

A quick glance at the newspaper at supper alerted me to the mess I had entered. Heathrow's new Terminal 5 was in total shut down. Over seventy British Airways flights had been cancelled already.

Oh well. I had a flight out the next morning, and I would get out of this place. Positive thinking isn't what it used to be.

Day Two—Saturday

I headed to my flight with Lufthansa and was told I had been taken off the flight as they were not boarding any passengers delayed by British Airways. I had to book a British Airways flight.

I was sick—literally sick—as I queued in an endless line of weary travellers trying to escape the prison of Heathrow Airport. I must have looked sick, as one of the helpers, who was directing the lineups, asked if I was OK.

I said, "*No*, I am not OK." I told him my story. He got on his phone and after a while, as we stood in line, he was able to book me a flight on Monday afternoon.

I said to myself, "OK if that is the best he could do." I thought I had better take it rather than jostle with the other prisoners for a seat that might never appear. So it was going to be two more days in London.

In the hotel room, I made extensive use of the phone to update Brian and my kids on my status.

I had no luggage during this time as all British Airways luggage was mixed up in the mess they had created. Upon inquiring, I found that my luggage was either in a huge pile at the terminal or perhaps even stored at a facility in Italy.

With the prospect of two more days in London, I caught a cab to a little village near the airport to get some clothes and a small suitcase. I thought of going into London, but I was too exhausted and upset. I ended up just lying on the bed in my hotel room and sulking.

Day Three—Sunday

On the off chance that there was a change in the situation, I got up early and checked the lineup at the airport. The lines weren't as bad, so I got queued up again and pleaded for an earlier flight to Canada as I needed to get home for my father's funeral.

The attendant took pity on me and browsed his system, determining that there was a flight leaving in the afternoon for Montreal. Then I could fly on to Toronto and to Regina.

"*Yes*, book it," I almost screamed.

I made some more phone calls from the hotel room and then went to check out so that I would be early for my flight. British Airways did cover the cost of the hotel room but not the phone calls, which totalled over three hundred pounds. I'm sure I could have found a smarter way to communicate, but when you are in such a state, economics is not at the top of your priority list.

In keeping with the rest of the journey, my flight to Montreal was late; however, it finally did take off, putting me in jeopardy of missing my connections to Toronto and Regina. I was edgy for the whole five-hour flight.

I guess I was right to be nervous. My flight to Toronto had already left when I arrived in Montreal, so I had to go back to a rebooking line. They could only get me out the next morning, so another night in a hotel courtesy of the airline.

Day Four—Monday

I got up early for my Toronto flight to witness a spring blizzard in Montreal. It wasn't bad enough to cancel flights, but we did board late and had to go through a de-icing process, delaying the take off and eventual landing in Toronto, thus missing my connection to Regina.

At the Toronto airport, I was back in another rebooking line where I was confirmed on an 8:00 p.m. flight to Regina and placed on a standby list for a 4:00 p.m. flight.

"It's noon, and I am stuck in another airport!" I shouted inside my head to avoid making a spectacle of myself.

The overbooked 4:00 p.m. flight left without me, allowing me to enjoy the wonders of Pearson International Airport for a total of eight hours. I did board the 8:00 p.m. flight and finally made it to Regina at 10:00 p.m. on Monday night after four days of hell.

Fortunately, I was still able to complete all the funeral arrangements and get started on the estate settlement before flying home in a normal fashion.

Here is how the BBC reported the British Airways computer disaster:

B B C NEWS

T5 chaos 'not BA's finest hour'

The chaos that marred Heathrow's Terminal 5 on its opening day, leaving many stranded overnight, "was not our finest hour" BA's boss has admitted.

British Airways' chief executive Willie Walsh accepted the debacle had affected the reputation of BA and of Britain.

More than 100 flights were cancelled on Thursday and Friday with another 54 flights on Saturday cancelled.

Airport operator BAA said it was working with BA to resolve the severe baggage problems.

A BAA spokesman said: "BAA's first duty is to passengers and airlines.

"Today at T5, we are focusing all our efforts on our work with British Airways to resolve baggage issues and to deliver a good service to passengers. Elsewhere at Heathrow, our terminals are working normally."

Mr Walsh said the situation was improving on Friday, but admitted the opening was not a success.

"We clearly disappointed a number of people and we sincerely apologise."

He said a "combination of factors" that they had been unable to "get on top of" had led to the disruption.

"British Airways has not delivered and we need to deliver," he said. "I am accepting responsibility, the buck stops with me."

He said: "Today has started much better," but added: "At this stage I still expect some cancellations tomorrow".

He told BBC Radio 4's World At One programme that if one of the numerous hold-ups - including staff car-parking problems, staff security screening and baggage delays - had happened "in isolation", then the resulting travel chaos would not have been so severe.

He described the baggage delays as "minor system problems" and said that as the system had undergone six months of testing "we should absolutely have done better".

"In isolation some of these problems were identified and we felt they had been addressed. There were some basic human errors made that compounded the problems."

Late on Friday the airline cancelled 54 flights to and from Heathrow on Saturday, while 293 flights remained on the schedule.

It followed the cancellation of 36 of Friday's flights from T5 and 36 to the terminal.

The airline advised customers to check its website, www.ba.com, for service updates.

Passengers could now check-in both hand and hold luggage.

The airline, which has sole use of T5, says it has drafted in extra staff and held meetings through the night to try to ease the problems that wrecked the terminal's first day.

Some stranded travellers spent the night on the floor of the new building.

The suspension of luggage check-in was not the only problem to hit passengers hoping to leave T5 on its opening day.

Earlier in the day BA announced that "initial teething problems" with car parking provision, delays in staff security screening and staff familiarisation had resulted in a backlog of baggage.

A further technical fault also meant seven flights left T5 without luggage on board.

Sources have also told the BBC that morale was low among staff.

One baggage handler told BBC News what should have been BA's greatest hour had "turned into a shambles the moment the doors opened".

"BA claimed 'staff familiarisation' was to blame. The staff, however, would blame the lack of training and the essential support that was promised," he said.

"During the inadequate training days prior to the opening, any staff questions were bounced back with 'I don't know' and 'It will be clear on the day'.

"Staff signage is non-existent and quite frankly, how are we expected to help customers if we are not helped first?"

BBC reporter Steve Rosenberg said on his flight from Berlin to Heathrow the captain warned passengers that "things haven't been going well at Heathrow, so keep your fingers crossed".

On arrival, there was a delay while ground staff were found to help park the plane, and there was no bus driver available to collect the disembarking passengers.

Once at the terminal door, there were further delays as a swipe card used to open it would not work. But our correspondent said his bags came through on the conveyor belt promptly.

The BBC's transport correspondent Tom Symonds said the backlog was caused by problems with the airport's luggage processing system.

An underground conveyor system had become clogged up, he said.

This was being blamed on staff failing to remove luggage quickly enough at the final unloading stage.

Passengers on Thursday's cancelled flights were offered £100 towards the cost of overnight accommodation by the airline, but travellers reported that local hotels were charging up to twice that figure.

David Frost, director general of the British Chambers of Commerce, said the "shambles" had sent a "depressing message to businesses around the world".

"This is a PR disaster at a time when London and the UK are positioning themselves as global players. We can only hope that this will provide a wake-up call as we gear ourselves up to host the Olympics in 2012."

Story from BBC NEWS:
http://news.bbc.co.uk/go/pr/fr/-
/2/hi/uk_news/7318337.stm

Published: 2008/03/28 18:42:13 GMT

Driving in Bangladesh

March 2012

We had the opportunity to visit Bangladesh in the spring of 2012 as a contingent of teachers who volunteered to help young Bangladeshi teachers develop their craft. The entire trip was the subject of another book, but this short story describes one of the highlights of our trip (or lowlights as the case may be).

This is not a factual account; it is a composite of various experiences during our many trips in the host van, reflecting comments and observations from several people in our group.

When your hands are covered in an objectionable substance, you can wash them with soap and water. When you have something you don't want in your eye, you can flush it out with eyewash. But what do you do to rid your mind of a moment of terror or, worse, several repeating moments of terror?

Although it was thirty-five degrees Celsius with unbearable humidity outside the van, it was twenty-two degrees and dry inside. Still rivers of sweat poured down my face, my hands trembled, and my stomach had knots that would make a sailor proud. I tried to enjoy the beauty of the countryside that was only rivaled by my Western Canadian home province. The river which separated us from Myanmar was lined with a variety of lush vegetation, including telephone-pole-straight coconut palms. The freshly harvested rice fields provided a checkerboard pattern reminding me of the Canadian prairie farmland, and the thatched-roof homes framed the narrow black ribbon which served as our roadway. Nominally it was a two-lane highway, but I have seen single car garages that are wider.

I glanced at Jamal, whose hands feathered the steering wheel in a casual manner. Not so much as a bead of moisture graced his brown forehead. His eagle eyes seldom left the road in front, but none of the chaos that we encountered seemed to have any effect on his calm disposition.

A man-powered three-wheeled rickshaw pushed its left wheel as close to the edge of the road as he dared, so as not to spill his three passengers reposed in the bonnet-covered seat behind him. A tom-tom (Bangladesh's three-wheeled equivalent of Thailand's four-wheeled tuk-tuks) was passing to the right of the rickshaw. Jamal was passing to the tom-tom's right, with his right wheel somewhere out of sight below us, obviously not in the ditch yet or we would have been tumbling along the shallow, green embankment, and we nine occupants of the vehicle would have served as feed for the free-roaming cows and goats.

If this wasn't enough to cause my palpitations, the oncoming bus, with its lights flashing, would be enough to finish me off. Driving on the left side of the road, rather than the right side, to which I was accustomed, added to my mental scramble. Somehow, a lazy dog sleeping in the middle of the road and two stray goats had sauntered out of the way seconds before we arrived at their space.

As I stared at the oncoming bus preparing to meet my fate, a miraculous straight line of vehicles formed on the left side of the road with our van in the lead, followed by the tom-tom with the rickshaw pulling up the rear. The bus, with his train-like horn filling the countryside, passed close enough that I could have written my name in the dust caking the side of the crowded commuter vehicle.

It's not as if we were travelling at a NASCAR-like speed; most North American drivers would be embarrassed to drive this slow, but at any speed a collision with such a bus would make us worthy of a fifth page column in any Canadian newspaper. Jamal never blinked as the scene unfolded time and time again. Yes, this wasn't a single occurrence; it was a constant collage of events over a three-hour drive to the southern part of Bangladesh.

The only reprieve was when we passed through a village with its inevitable marketplace filled with rickshaws and pedestrians, challenging Jamal's skills, weaving at the pace of one of the local tortoises on the beach. These were the moments when I could look out the window and take in some of the wondrous cultural scenes gracing my vision: hot peppers laid out to dry, a butcher chopping at a carcass hanging from a yardarm, piles of raw rice, and unrecognizable local fruits and vegetables, not to mention the colourful people in unfamiliar garb sitting, walking, and sometimes laying on or near the dirty roadway.

With my innards bouncing from the rollercoaster-like highway, we pulled to a stop at our destination next to the vast Bay of Bombay. These images of terror were etched on my retina as I walked to deliver a day's worth of training to our beneficiaries with my cohorts. As the images began to fade, I knew I would have a new set of fresh images to replace the old ones on our three-hour journey home later in the day. No amount of soap or eyewash would rid my mind of those images.

Here is how the news media characterizes Bangladesh's roads:

Bangladesh's road accidents take heavy toll on poor – and on the economy. Road crashes disproportionately affect poor families, and cost Bangladesh almost as much as it receives in foreign aid.

Syed Zain Al-Mahmood in Dhaka guardian.co.uk, Wednesday 22 August 2012 13.00 BST

Bangladesh has one of the highest accident rates in the world. Photograph: Syed Zain Al-Mahmood Hajera Begum, a farmer from the Munshiganj district in central Bangladesh, was taking vegetables to market with her husband Solaiman when the pickup truck they were riding in was hit by a bus. Five people were killed, including Solaiman. Hajera, who suffered broken ribs, lost not only her husband but also her land and her livelihood.

"My family used to be well off," said Hajera. "We had quite a bit of land, and we made a good living off it. But since my husband died, I have struggled. I have had to sell much of our land. Some of it was grabbed by local gangs. I am now worried for my future and that of my two children."

More than 4,000 people die on Bangladesh's roads every year. The country has one of the highest rates in the world, with more than 85 deaths for every 10,000 registered motor vehicles. That's around 50 times higher than the rate in most western countries.

Traffic accidents strike deadly blows to poor families like the Begums, and they also suck billions out of Bangladesh's economy. According to the World Health Organisation (WHO), road traffic injuries cause a loss of about 2% of GDP in Bangladesh, or about £1.2bn annually. This is almost equal to the total foreign aid received in a fiscal year. The losses include direct and indirect expenses, such as medical costs, insurance loss, property damage, family income losses and traffic congestion.

Experts say crashes disproportionately affect the poor, making road safety a vital issue for economic development. "Road traffic crashes are like the constant drip-drip of blood haemorrhaging from the body," says Professor Mazharul Hoque, an expert at the Accident Research Institute, a road safety research centre within the Bangladesh University of Engineering and Technology. "Road accidents kill and injure people who are young and productive, and therefore have a hidden development impact."

Case studies in Bangladesh found that poor families were more likely than those better off to lose their head of household and suffer immediate economic effects as a result of road traffic injuries. The loss of earnings, together with medical, funeral and legal bills, can have a ruinous effect on a family's finances, according to the WHO's world report on road traffic injury prevention.

Another study, carried out by the Centre for Injury Prevention and Research Bangladesh in 2001, sheds light on the huge burden traffic accidents place on Bangladesh's healthcare system. It found that one-fifth of injury patients in primary and secondary level hospitals across the country had been involved in a traffic accident. More than two-thirds of victims were males aged between 18 and 45.

"Trauma treatment is exceedingly expensive and does represent a huge drain on healthcare resources," says Valerie Taylor, a British physiotherapist who founded the Centre for the Rehabilitation of the Paralysed in Savar, near Dhaka, in 1979.

Bangladesh is trying to modernise its road network, but population and commerce continue to outpace transport infrastructure, turning roads – devoid of proper safety measures – into death traps.

Modernising highways is not necessarily the answer, says Hoque. Better roads, he adds, are not necessarily safer roads. "Traditional road design aimed at reducing the number of crashes by widening and straightening roads," he says. "But that has no impact on the rate of death and disability because people simply start to drive faster. We must adopt the internationally accepted systemic approach to road safety, taking into consideration vehicles, roads and road users."

At the invitation of the ministry of communications, the International Road Assessment Programme (Irap) last year carried out assessments on the Dhaka-Sylhet and the Dhaka-Mymensingh highways, identifying design and maintenance flaws that are contributing to the growing toll of death and disability.

"We don't want gold-plated roads," says Greg Smith, Asia-Pacific regional director of Irap, who led the study. "With a scientific approach, sometimes a coat of white paint will save lives ... We know how people are killed, and what can be done to stop it. All we need is the political will to implement these countermeasures."

In recognition of the burden road accidents place on developing economies, the UN declared 2011-20 the decade of action for road safety. Experts say policymakers in countries such as Bangladesh must stop thinking of road safety as a mere transport issue and recognise it as a public health and sustainable development problem.

"I get so angry sometimes," says Taylor. "The other day on the Savar road I saw a child with his head cracked open like a nut. What a waste! In the UK, school children get the 'Look right, look left, then right again' message drilled into them at an early age. Such a simple campaign could save so many young lives in Bangladesh."

Living in China

We had the good fortune to live in China for a year. See my book on Amazon.com:

Living In China: Our Year in Shenyang

http://www.amazon.com/Living-China-Our-Year-Shenyang-ebook/dp/B00JDPZFBW

Some of the following stories are contained in that book but are interesting enough to retell here.

Down on the Farm
January 2003

Three days and two nights almost defined our year in China. We weren't sure what we were getting into by accepting Robin's (Cui Ji or little chicken in Chinese) invitation to his family farm. This was to be the richest experience of our time in China. We couldn't believe how many memories were crammed into this seventy-hour trip. Below is the experience, broken into events, rather than chronology.

Getting There

On January 16, 2003, in the middle of winter with temperatures in the minus twenties Celsius, we boarded a train with our friend Robin to visit his family on a small farm near a village in northeast China. Robin was a novice at English, but was working very hard at it. He would be our only form of communication for the entire trip.

Robin's family had never seen a foreigner before, so this was to be quite an experience for everyone. The family consisted of a mother and father (both about our age) son (Robin, twenty-three) and daughter (Hong, fifteen) plus Gramma (eighty-six). There is a law in China that each family can only have one child. One exception is for farm families, who may have two children. Robin's parents went to the limit.

As always happened, there was a young fellow on the train who was learning English, and he wanted to practice his English the entire trip. He was a university student in Shenyang at a different school from ours, and he was going home for the Spring Festival.

When we arrived in the small town after three hours travelling soft-class on the train, we were assaulted by a barrage of vendors, especially unlicensed taxi drivers. One of them, a lady driver, attached herself to Robin while he went to buy our return tickets. You cannot buy roundtrip tickets so we had to purchase our return ticket at our destination. As it turns out, this train station was too small for the "real" trains to stop to pick up passengers, only drop them off, so we could only purchase tickets for the cattle-car trains. We were anxious to see what that experience would be like when traveling hard-class.

When we left the train station, the lady was pulling Robin to her car for our journey to the farm. Rochelle became quite annoyed and belligerent at the lady's behaviour and refused to take her offer of transportation. Rochelle marched to a legitimate taxi and got in. Robin was confused and the lady driver was annoyed, but Rochelle got her way and we were off in the real taxi.

The drive started out on a very civil paved highway. However, as we approached a toll road, the taxi driver took some side roads to avoid paying the toll. The side roads were merely pathways with hardly enough room for a car and a pedestrian at the same time, let alone two vehicles. Pedestrians did not have the right of way, so they had to jump out of the way when the driver honked, which he did most of the trip.

I started to ask Robin what happened when two vehicles met on the road, but before he could answer, I found out. A large three-wheeled truck approached us. It was debatable who was going to give in. Fortunately there was a small swelling in the road and we were able to pass. This happened several times during the twenty-minute drive.

The Farm House

We arrived at the home, which was quite a respectable farm home, but not in the same category as a Canadian farm house. With five rooms, it was a large enough home, but two of those rooms were purely for storage. One room was an entrance way and storage for the motor bike, and it doubled as the kitchen. Quite a combination.

The living quarters consisted of two large rooms, one of which was the living room, bedroom, and eating room all combined. The other was a bedroom and storage room. Where was the bathroom? You know the toilet, bath/shower, sink, etc.? Our expectations were not high, which was a good thing given what we would discover.

The floor of the home was bare concrete. This made it easier to clean up cigarette butts, peanut shells, and other items that accumulated from daily living.

The family had lived in this house for about ten years. The father built it when the old house became inadequate. The old one was of a similar size, but was made of mud.

We could see that there were only two beds in the house. Based on my accounting background, I determined that there were five family members and two guests, totaling seven people. We were curious about how this would work itself out.

Open Doors

As in all rural communities, Canada or China, everyone knows each other.

There is no need to lock the doors. What is mine is yours. So, while we were visiting, many of the neighbors dropped in, literally walked in, to look at the foreigners. Some would just sit on the couch, have a smoke (which was just thrown on the floor when done), smile, and then leave. Some would check us out, pay their respects to Gramma, and be on their way. One fellow came in while we were having supper and was asked to join us. At first he said no; he had already eaten. But then he changed his mind, saying this might be his only chance to sit and eat with a foreigner. None of this was done in a way to make us feel uncomfortable. In fact we felt quite special and flattered. We joked with Robin that we felt like VIPs. He said that with our presence, he and his family were now also celebrities in this close-knit community.

Beds and Sleeping

The two beds—connected, but separated by a wall—were part of a traditional Chinese "kang." These beds were made of wood and mud, but covered with vinyl so you didn't see any of the materials. They were hollow underneath to accommodate the primitive, but elaborate and creative, heating system. In the kitchen there was a wood-burning fireplace/stove. This stove heated the water for the hot water heating system in the living room, and it also provided the heat for the *kang*. The airflow system was such that the heat from the fire was drawn under the beds and out the chimney. This provided for a very warm bed in which to sleep. Mother stoked the fire before bed time and the bed stayed warm until morning.

But how do you fit seven people into two beds? Well as it turns out, being a guest does have its privileges. Rochelle and I were assigned the large *kang* in the living room. This was the bed that also substituted as a kitchen counter and seating at the supper table, as well as a place to sit and visit during the cold of winter, as you could stay warm with the heat emanating from below.

What about the other five people? Mother, Father, Gramma, Robin, and Hong all got the other *kang*. These large beds could accommodate up to eight people, properly spaced. I gathered that intimacy and privacy did not exist in rural China.

The Bohai Sea

17/01/2003

The community was located a few miles from the Bohai Sea. This is the same body of water from which we saw the Great Wall, but on the other side of the water. Rochelle loves the sea, so we had to make a trip to the sea on the Friday of our trip. It was a cold and windy day. Robin's father said it was probably too cold to go to the sea today, but we were from Canada and could take the cold. So we called a taxi and Robin took us to the sea. With the wind, the temperature at the sea was at least ten degrees colder than inland. We made the long walk down an endless stairway to the beach. When we arrived at the seaside, I felt like I was back in the Arctic. The wind was howling and the ice extended about half a kilometer before you could see open water. A couple of quick pictures to prove that we were there and we hopped back in the taxi. Father knows best.

Farmer's Market

On the Saturday, there was an open-air market in a local village, about a fifteen-minute walk from the house. The weather was cold, but pleasant. Although the market was crowded, it actually had far fewer people than we were used to in Shenyang. If we felt like fish out of water in Shenyang, the feeling was exaggerated tenfold in this community. People looked at us (especially Rochelle) as if we were from outer space; they would nudge each other and point, appearing to be nervous, almost afraid, of our presence. Not many "hellos" from this crowd. Most of these people had seldom left their community and had never seen a foreigner other than on TV. Rochelle bought a sweater for fifteen yuan and a few gifts for our host family. Then we headed back to the farm house.

Toilet

We didn't have high expectations for bathroom facilities and were warned by others that the toilet would be outside. Well, it was. There was no running water in the home, and that means no toilet, no sinks, no bath or shower. We were told by someone that Chinese farmers bathe twice, once when they are born and once when they die. I could see where that story came from.

The toilet was about fifty meters from the back door. Quite a walk on a dark, cold, windy winter night. You first had to pass the three large geese that stood guard near the back door. The geese expected some attention each time you passed, as they make quite a noise and they announced to the world that you were headed to the toilet. There must have been an invisible fence that kept the geese from escaping because they never strayed from their assigned space.

The Toilet Outside

The "building" that housed the toilet consisted of a loose stack of brick and a tin roof. There were lots of holes for ventilation, and there was no door. Inside there was a hole dug in the dirt, and on either side of the hole was a wooden slat on which to place your feet as you squatted over the hole. You had a good view of the medical condition of anyone who had used the facility prior to your entrance. This was obviously an earlier design of the public washrooms we saw elsewhere in China.

The Toilet Inside

We kept our fluid consumption to a minimum as getting up in the middle of the night for a trip to the toilet was not appealing. Rochelle had already mastered the art of the Chinese toilet, but I never became quite as adept.

The Farm

Robin's father owned (at least I think he owned) about five acres of land. He appeared to be one of the more progressive farmers in the community as he was always trying new methods, and other farmers came to him for advice.

He was about fifty years old and had been farming for many years. He had a grade five education, but was an avid learner with his living quarters filled with many books about farming. He started out as a young man in a factory making tofu. After that he was a vendor buying and selling clothes. I'm not sure how, but he ended up getting some land and planting some fruit trees.

Now he had two greenhouses—one for grapes and one for pear trees—as well as outdoor apple trees, peach trees, and other assorted fruit trees. The fruit was grown to sell, but they grew lots of other things for their own use, including peanuts.

The father found that his fruit trees were far more productive if there were more bees nearby, so he started farming bees. He didn't harvest the honey, just relied on the bees to fertilize the flowers of the fruit trees. He had developed such an interest in bees that he did a lot of research on them. He showed us some reading he was doing (in Chinese of course) on bee farming in Alberta.

The farm did not have running water, but there was a well with an electric pump to supply drinking water and water for the plants.

He maintained two large greenhouses that were not used for growing during the winter, but rather housed the dormant plants in order to preserve them for the summer growing season. During the night, the greenhouses were covered with a straw curtain to keep in the heat and protect the dormant plants. In the morning, the farmer went up on the roof of the greenhouses and switched on an electric motor to lift the covering. This was quite progressive, as other farmers performed a similar function by hand.

I didn't find out what his annual income was, but Robin told me that a top farmer would make about twenty thousand yuan per year (about four thousand dollars Canadian). Given Robin's annual cost for school of about fifteen thousand yuan, I could see the value that people placed on their children and their education.

Robin did not want to be a farmer and wanted to get off the land. His father also felt this was the right thing to do. There was a hierarchy or class system in the country that we never completely figured out. At the bottom of the pile are the peasants who own nothing and eke out a living by working the land for someone else. Farmers, like Robin's father, were just above the peasant. Ranking above that was what Robin called workers, which I think meant factory workers and the like. These three groups made up the majority of the population. There was a very small middle class and then the wealthy class.

The total cost of our three-day excursion was about forty Canadian dollars, but you could never buy such an experience and very few people ever had such an opportunity—we felt privileged.

English/Chinese Lesson

There isn't a lot to do on a Chinese farm in the winter, so we spent a lot of time sitting on the *kang* reading and visiting. Visiting was quite a challenge because of the language barrier. Robin was a very avid learner of English, but his English was not strong enough to carry on long conversations. Also his skills as a translator were stretched to the limit during our visit. By the end of the day he was mentally exhausted from trying to keep things going.

On the Friday, Robin wanted to practice his pronunciation. So he took out some English books and had Rochelle help him. We had gotten good at understanding him, but his pronunciation required more work. The rest of the family watched intently as Rochelle helped him with some of the more difficult pronunciations. Many of our language sounds do not have a Chinese equivalent—for example "V" and "R."

01/16/2003

Then Rochelle said it was her turn and Robin worked with Rochelle and her books on the Chinese language. Just as there are English sounds with no Chinese equivalents, there are Chinese sounds with no English equivalents. Rochelle was just as competent at her Chinese sounds as Robin was with his English sounds. The family found the simultaneous English/Chinese lesson amusing.

Rochelle's account of the farm visit—in her words:

Cooking

There is a big pot and the smaller pot in the kitchen on a rustic stove, stoked with wood and corn stalks. This is where all the cooking takes place. Under the pot is the fire. This fire also heats the kang in the next room and supplies the heat to the register.

Three times a day fuel is added to the furnace.

The big pot is used to cook, like a big steamer. A rack is put over the boiling water, similar to how we are cooking with our steamer. Then different pots with the different foods are put on to cook. It really is quite effective and efficient.

First Meal

We arrived at the farm around 12:30 pm. Time for lunch, the main meal of the day.

There was no table that we could see, so we sat on the kang and visited as lunch was being prepared. When the food was ready, Robin brought out from the other room a fold out table and the food was brought in.

Of course the traditional bowls of rice were part of the meal. Other things were not so normal. Have you ever eaten silk worm cocoons? Well I have, now. They're very salty and like a liver paste. Blood sausage. Sour cabbage, noodles, eggs and tomatoes, pork and other stuff. All delicious and cooked on the one big cooking pot.

Making Dumplings

While we were at the farm, Robin's Mom and sister decided to make dumplings for us. Only honoured guests ever see fresh made dumplings.

The production line was set up on the "kang" (our bed).

I decided I should try to help and that is when the fun began.

First Mom tried to show me how to do it, then the sister tried. Finally Grandma joined in the lesson and also tried to show me. The trouble was folding them correctly and making them the correct shape. I obviously was a slow learner. There was lots of laughter at my dumplings, which were set in a special pile. Only some of mine made it to the main pile. I thought mine looked just like the others, but they didn't seem to pass the "gramma test."

Later on that day, we were asked if we wanted a snack. We said yes, and my dumplings were cooked and served. But no one else joined in. The rest of the family didn't seem to need a snack at that time. So Brian and I ate my dumplings, which I thought were delicious. The "good" dumplings were served the next morning for breakfast. Were mine part of the "good" dumplings? I couldn't tell, but maybe the rest of the family could.

Chicken for Lunch

On our second morning, we were asked what we liked to eat. Brian mentioned that we really like chicken.

Robin's father disappeared and then returned with a live rooster in his arms. He had gone out and bought it from a neighbor. It was still quite alive and

looked at us, not seeming to know its fate. It was a pretty bird and I was ready to make a pet of it. You can tell I'm not from the farm.

First Dad showed the chicken around and it was inspected by Mom. Next it was weighed. Then the ax came out. Time to say good-bye to our friendly rooster.

But wait, the phone rings and it is for Dad. So rooster in hand, he talks on the phone. No sound from the bird. A stay of execution, a reprieve.

The phone call is finished, so we once again say good-bye to the rooster. Life (death?) on the farm.

Hot Pot

Hot pot meals are only for very special occasions, like New Year's and, of course, when you have foreign visitors. We were extremely lucky and were treated to two hot pot dinners.

The hot pot "cooker" is put on the fold out table and coal is used to boil the broth in the pot. When the broth is boiling, all sorts of things are put into the broth. Oysters, shrimp, beef, pork, chicken, onions, lettuce, anything.

Then everyone digs in, with chop sticks and fishes things out of the pot. Different sauces such a peanut and a hot sauce are used to dip the goodies in. It is so good.

Hot pot meals are very social occasions. You do not eat in a hurry. You only eat a little at a time. It is a time to socialize and visit with friends. It is a wonderful experience.

We had been to quite a few hot pot restaurants since being in China but this was the best hot pot I have ever tasted. Maybe it was the atmosphere and the special people that we had at the table with us.

Grandma

For me, one of the highlights of our visit to the farm was Grandma. As is the custom, she lives with her oldest son's family. She is held with great respect and with high regard by all the family members.

She was eighty-six years old and not able to read or write. Her marriage, in about 1933, was prearranged. The story is told that she was very beautiful and was carried into her marriage on a covered platform. When she first saw her husband, the day of the wedding, she thought he was too short and homely. But the marriage lasted over 60 years and produced five children.

She had never met a foreigner before, so at first she was a little hesitant and uncertain about us. She just observed us, from a distance. But that did not last for long. Her mind was lively and quick. Soon she was asking Robin to ask us questions and the communication began.

For some reason, she took a liking to us and we now were very honoured to have a "Chinese Mother." She asked Robin, "When are they coming back again?" She wanted us to visit her again.

Grandma does not leave the farm. She has never been to a restaurant. Her world is the farm and her family. She will sit cross-legged (lotus style) for hours. I sat with her for a while one day. She held my hands and looked at them. She told me I was too thin. I must eat more.

Every day she carries in dried corn stalks to heat the "kang" in what is actually her bedroom, she shared with her granddaughter. She was able to make it to the outdoor bathroom, which is quite an accomplishment in itself. Down a plank, by the geese, along a dirt path.

A moment I will treasure, is sitting on the "kang" with grandma and her showing me her tiny feet which had been bound as a young girl; and then comparing the size of our feet. She was quite fascinated at my small feet and that they never had been bound.

She is an intriguing and awesome lady. At eighty-six she still had a twinkle in her eyes, a curious mind and an interest in life. Oh, if only I could understand Chinese.

I would sit and listen as she talked about her life; what she has seen and experienced and what she has lived through.

Hard Class

Our train was leaving at 3:55 p.m. on Saturday. Robin's father arranged for a cab to come and get us at about three o'clock, which would get us to the station by three thirty. The cab arrived shortly before three and we all piled in, including Robin and his father, who insisted on seeing us to the train station. We no sooner got the bags stowed in the trunk and were comfortably seated when the driver, who had been on his cell phone, ordered us all out. Apparently he had promised another passenger a ride at that time, but insisted he would only be a couple of minutes.

We went back into the house and waited. There were not many taxis in this community and they were not usually very close to the farm, so we didn't have much choice but to wait. As the minutes ticked away, Rochelle and I contemplated spending a third night on the farm due to missing the train. Given the royal treatment we had received, that would not be a disaster, but we were looking forward to a shower and a bathroom.

Approaching three thirty, the driver made it back and we were all off. Down the same back roads, avoiding the toll road, from where we had come; the clock still ticking to our 3:55 departure. There was an old open truck ahead of us, carrying some kind of farm stuff and going at a snail's pace. In spite of the taxi driver constantly leaning on his horn, the farmer refused to pull over to one of the side roads to let us by. We had to crawl behind him until he turned off to a side road.

Finally we reached the town. But the main road was blocked with some kind of machinery. The driver found some back roads through town and we reached the train station with about four minutes to spare. It was a rush to get on board before the train departed.

Robin's father refused to let us pay for the taxi. He was going to make sure we got excellent treatment right to the end. Robin and his father carried our bags right to the door of the train and saw us off. Robin insisted that we call him when we got home, as he was quite worried for our well-being in this strange land.

This was our first experience on a rush-seating train. On this type of transportation, there are as many seats as on our regular trains, but no assigned seats and an unlimited number of passengers. So we put our bags on the overhead racks and stood in the aisle for our multi-hour trip. Given that this was a hard-class train that stopped in every small community, it would be a much longer return trip than our journey to the farm.

The aisles were full of people, but that didn't stop the food vendors from rolling their carts up and down the aisle selling anything from full meals to snacks, drinks, and beer. They just pushed their way through and people had to jump out of the way or be driven over.

Shortly into our trip, as was predicted in some of our culture books, a gentleman stood up and let Rochelle have his seat. In spite of her protesting, he insisted. I stood for another fifteen minutes before the gentleman across from Rochelle stood up to give me his seat. I objected as well, but it was his stop anyway, so I sat down. We now each had a window seat for the rest of the trip.

Unlike our other journeys, there was no one who spoke English on this trip. We were the subject of much staring, as foreigners did not travel on this form of economy fare (the cost was nineteen yuan each or less than four dollars Canadian).

They did not announce the stops (and there were many) on this train, so we were ever-vigilant to see some familiar sights to signal our arrival at the Shenyang North Station. There was also a South Station, so we didn't want to get it wrong. Nor did we want to see the next province north, which is even colder.

When we had travelled over three hours, we reached a stop that looked like the South Station of Shenyang. If I was right, then the next stop was ours. If I was wrong, then we might have a different adventure. I used my not-so-extensive vocabulary and perfect pronunciation (as I am often told) to ask the people next to us if this was the South station and if the next station was the North station of Shenyang. I'm sure they said yes, but they looked puzzled as we grabbed our bags and went to wait at the exit for our stop.

I guess there was some breakdown in communication, as it turned out not to be Shenyang, which meant standing in the aisle among the pushing, shoving, and vendor carts for another couple of stops. We continued to be the subject of much discussion and staring from the travelers as we came to our final stop at the Shenyang North Station. After fighting off illegal taxi services, we found our way to a legitimate driver and made our way home, to the bathroom and a shower before bed.

Here is another excerpt from my book *Living in China*, **about our year in the northeast city of Shenyang.**

http://www.amazon.com/Living-China-Our-Year-Shenyang-ebook/dp/B00JDPZFBW

Chinese Medicare
February 2003

Just as our Chinese Spring Festival holiday was starting, I developed what appeared to be a pimple or growth on my left eyelid. I decided to see if it would go away on its own like most pimples do. It did go down in size but never really disappeared. I found that the vision in that eye seemed to get worse—a bit blurred, even with my glasses on.

Then during the holidays, my glasses broke, so I spent most of the holidays without my glasses and just ignored the blur.

When we returned from the holidays, I put on my old set of glasses and still had the blurred vision in my left eye—the pimple was still there.

We asked our friend Mary to take me to the doctor to have it checked out. In China, a trip to the doctor meant a trip to the hospital. There was no public healthcare of any kind, so anyone going for medical attention must pay for all services and medication at the time of service.

We picked up Mary in a cab about eight fifteen in the morning and went to the hospital. Mary was essential to this endeavor, as there was little chance of finding anyone who could speak English.

The first stop in the hospital was the cashier. There you have to choose if you are going to see a specialist or a general practitioner. The specialist cost 18 RMB and the GP cost 14 RMB (1 RMB = 20 cents Canadian). We chose the specialist and took our receipt to the eye doctor ward.

Even though people had to pay from their pockets, the hospital was very busy. (Remember, the average wage in Shenyang was 10,000 RMB per year). We saw through our entire visit to the hospital that line-ups meant nothing—queuing was as foreign in the hospital as it was at the concert hall at New Year's. If you didn't push to the front of the line, you didn't get served.

With receipt in hand, I waited my turn. The first stop was the eye chart. I'm not sure why I had to do this, as I didn't come for a vision test. I dutifully pointed to the direction of the "E" as I was requested. The nurse wrote something on my chart, and I was off to the next stop.

We (Mary was with me every step of the way) went to a little room to see the real doctor. There was a line-up out the door, which we dutifully joined, however, after seeing people push their way to the front to get immediate service, Mary did the same and we got our turn—even if it was out of turn.

The doctor looked at my eyes and said that I needed an operation to remove the pimple. But she decided to have a closer look, so she took us to a room where she and another doctor examined my eyes. I was told I had two problems. One was the pimple and the other was something inside my left eye.

This meant another examination, so off to the cashier to pay for the next phase. This time it was 40 RMB. With my receipt, I was granted admission to another examination room. They put me in some kind of computer diagnostic chair where I had to look at a light with my left eye, while clicking a button every time I saw a small flash of light anywhere on the screen. This seemed to go on forever. The technician took a printout of what had just happened and said that there was nothing wrong with my eye.

So back to the original doctor, push to the front of the line, and tell her the news. She said that I still needed to have the operation to remove the pimple and it would only take ten minutes.

With some reluctance, I agreed. This meant another trip to the cashier—117 RMB this time. Now back to the doctor again. She said we also needed the medication for the operation and she wrote out a prescription for which we first had to pay at the cashier (4 RMB) and then pick it up at the dispensary.

Now we headed off to the operating room with the appropriate receipts and medication, which included the freezing that I had to bring from the pharmacy. The operating room was housed behind a locked door at which I waited until someone appeared to signal my next step. I then shoved my paperwork and medication at them and waited until I was called for my operation.

I was finally called after about a twenty-minute wait. The locked door opened, and I sat on a small stool where I had to put plastic bags over my shoes— for sanitary purposes, no doubt. From this point I was on my own; Mary and Rochelle had to wait outside. I was then escorted to an operating table where I lay on my back. I still had my parka and boots on, but my boots were duly covered with plastic bags.

Now the scary part. The doctor started to dab my left eye with liquid. Then he covered my face with a cloth that had a hole for my one eye. I was very nervous at this point, and he started to do all kinds of things with my eye. Although there was no real pain, I felt like he was sticking a needle right through my eyeball. There was lots of pushing and twisting and then finally, after what seemed like an eternity (maybe five minutes), he sent me on my way with instructions to keep my eye covered for ten minutes, not to get water on it for the next day, and to return the next morning to have him check it out.

This must have been a common operation, as Rochelle said the next person in line was a young lady with exactly the same ailment.

The time was now just after ten o'clock in the morning. The whole process took about ninety minutes from front to back. And I felt good enough to go out shopping. We stopped at an eyeglass store where they fixed my glasses free of charge. I removed my patch and was able to see, although it felt like I had sand in my eye. I think he must have cut out the growth from under the eyelid.

The doctor said I should come back the next day to have it checked, so we picked up Mary the next morning and went back to the hospital. The first stop was the cashier to pay for my visit. Then back to the doctor who, after browsing my receipt, looked at my eye. Everything seemed to be well and he prescribed some medication.

The medication exercise was complicated. First I had to take my prescription to the line-up at the pharmacy window where they gave me a price. Next I lined up at the cashier to pay the stated price. Then I took my receipt back to the line-up at the pharmacy window, and they dispensed my medication. Total cost for the eye drops and salve was 17 RMB.

With a bandage over my eye, I wondered if I would ever see out of that eye again. However, by the next day, the bandage had fallen off, and I was back to normal.

For a communist country, China was a very free enterprise system—even with their healthcare system.

Ding Dong Dandong
August 2005

The wait for the birth of my first grandson saw me half a world away, vacationing in China in an attempt to recreate the magic of the year Rochelle and I spent living in the country that Mao created. Dandong is a Chinese city on the Yalu River across which you can gaze at the stunted people of North Korea.

Our three-star hotel was more than adequate and was situated next to the railway station where we had arrived, making it unnecessary to deal with the hordes of taxi drivers and hawkers. Sitting in our comfortable surroundings, I browsed the hotel guide and began to laugh out loud at the lack of skill, or perhaps the sense of humour, of the translator who had transcribed all of the items from the adjacent Chinese characters to almost readable English.

Any grammar and spelling errors are the responsibility of the translator. Italics are my editorial.

> "The central vault, with diameter of 5 metres, provides a good place for singing with perfect sound effect."

I guess they assume you are a bad singer if they plan on putting you in a vault.

> Notice to guests:
> "The price here is the cost of one day, which is based on the area, type, and lacation of the rooms. Inquire the price before enter the hotel and pay off all the price and other service fee on feceiving the ill."

Will it make you sick?

> "No other person is allowed to stay for the night. No transforing of changing one's own bed or room."

Don't you dare change your bed.

Check out some of the dishes on the room service menu:

> "The taste is small to fry."

If it's too small to fry isn't it too small to eat?

"Onion explodes"

Don't get too close.

"The sauce explodes eight fish."

I think I would prefer the exploding onion.

"Elbow son rape"

Is this a food or a service?

"Fuck Huang the flower the fish"

Is this a food or game for consenting adults?

"Burn the eggplant"

At least it doesn't explode.

"Wood must yellow"

Before or after eating it?

"Meat burns the cloud bean"

So don't let them touch.

Or how about the drink menu:

"The green river in fucks"

> "Remit the source fruit juice"

> "Gold benefit fruit vinegar"

I think I'll stick with bottled water.

Then when it is time to leave:

> "Check out time as the noon
> 12:00 ago."

Am I late?

> "The child under twelve years
> of age lives together with
> parents, needing not to pay
> moreover."

What if he lives apart?

> "If adove Building price and
> board room prices contain
> adjustment, forgive not another
> circular."

I will never forgive another circular.

But never fear:

> "The hotel is patrolled by
> secruity guards. In case of
> doubt or insecurity, contact

the security deparment."

...or if you are just feeling a little down.

There were many more confusing statements in the hotel guide that defied comment.

Living in the Middle East

From 2003 to 2014, we had the unforgettable experience of living in the Middle East. Our first-seven-plus years were in the desert city of Al Ain, not far from the international metropolis of Dubai. We then moved to Doha, Qatar, just after that peninsular nation was awarded hosting the 2022 FIFA World Cup.

Although this period of time contains many cultural experiences that will be the subject of at least one future book, here are a few experiences that stand out.

Visa Run *October 2003*

Upon our initial arrival in the UAE, I picked up my work visa at the airport as I entered the country. The college where I was employed arranged for it to be waiting for me upon arrival. Rochelle, however, was instructed to enter on a standard visit visa. Once my resident visa was finalized, I could sponsor Rochelle for her resident visa. At that time, visit visas from favoured countries such as Canada were for a period of sixty days.

Once the time came for Rochelle's resident visa to be processed, we discovered that the most important document to the process, our marriage certificate, was not complete. I had the document notarized and stamped by a lawyer before our departure from Canada, but apparently I was supposed to submit it to be authenticated by the Canadian government and then stamped by the UAE embassy in Canada. Without the necessary purple stamp on the back of the certificate, the UAE government would not recognize its authenticity. This would have relegated us to "living in sin," which is an offense punishable by jail in a Muslim country.

Walid, our visa officer at the college, said he knew a way of getting it fixed, but it was going to take some time. However, Rochelle's sixty-day visit visa would expire before the process was complete. Thus, the need for a visa run.

A visa run is taking a trip to another country, getting an exit stamp in your passport, and re-entering the original country with a new visit visa. This process is done all over the world, often by those working illegally in a country and unable to get an employment visa. It is so common, in fact, that a subset of the tourism industry is devoted to supporting this practice.

Not long before Rochelle found herself in this predicament, we discovered that an airline flying out of Fujairah on the west coast of the UAE provided this service. All you had to do was show up at the airport, buy a cheap ticket for the plane that was sitting on the tarmac, get stamped by passport control to prove you were leaving the country, and board the plane. Once full, the plane would taxi to the end of the runway, turn around, and then taxi back to the terminal without ever having left the ground. Passengers would then disembark and enter the terminal to be stamped with a new visit visa by the same official that had bid them adieu only moments before.

Governments tend to turn a blind eye to such practices, but this particular service was getting to be too much of a joke even for the UAE's less-than-efficient immigration officials. They ordered this visa run to cease.

So Rochelle had to actually leave the country and get stamped out of the UAE, and then stamped in and out of another country before being stamped back in upon arrival in the UAE. The college agreed to pay for Rochelle's travel, which involved a ninety-minute taxi ride from Al Ain to Dubai and then a flight to another country. Fortunately for us, the chosen country was neighbouring Qatar rather than the common visa run destination of Kish Island off the coast of Iran where it was not unusual for bad things to happen to people, especially women, on a visa run. Recently, a former FBI agent went missing on the island, never to be seen again.

At the Dubai airport, Rochelle was stamped out of the country by immigration control and boarded a flight for Doha, Qatar, about a twenty-minute flight across the Arabian Gulf. Once in Doha, immigration officials stamped her into the country. She then entered the airport arrivals area where she turned around to get stamped out of Qatar by the same official that stamped her in. She then boarded the same plane that had brought her over the Gulf and returned to Dubai to be stamped in with a new sixty-day visit visa.

This new visa gave Walid enough time to process our certificate and get Rochelle her resident visa.

We repeared this process several years later for our niece who came to Al Ain and was working illegally while waiting for her employer to process her visa. By this time visit visas were only thirty days, and each month we took a drive to the Oman border where we would get her stamped out of the UAE, stamped in and out of Oman, and stamped back into the UAE with a new visit visa. We would always take advantage of these trips to visit different parts of Oman. After four visa runs, Melissa finally got her resident visa.

Hospital Holiday
July 2010

The summer of 2010 saw us heading into our final holiday as residents of the United Arab Emirates. We would be sorry to leave our home for the past seven-plus years in the desert city of Al Ain, but the work environment had become too much for either of us to tolerate.

I could have handled more if it hadn't been for Rochelle's predicament. For almost two years, Rochelle had been the reluctant manager of the department at our college with the most faculty and the most students. She was neither qualified for nor interested in doing the job of Chair of the Work Readiness Program. However, she did an excellent job of excelling in an unmanageable situation. Perhaps her success was because she didn't really want the job and would have liked nothing more than to be relieved of her onerous duties. The stress had taken its toll on her health, and we were looking forward to a summer of rest and relaxation before returning for the final stretch.

I had just received a very lucrative offer to move to Doha, and although it would be easy for Rochelle to find meaningful work there, the plan was to have her relax for a few months before seeking work. We still had to return to Al Ain after the summer for one last semester before my Doha contract commenced in January.

Our summer plan was to start with a few days in Atlanta to visit my older son and then travel to Calgary to see my younger son and Rochelle's daughter. Then, we would go to Chicago where my older son would travel for his marriage vow renewal, and I would also attend a writer's conference to hone my skills. Following that, we would spend a few more days in Atlanta before spending our final month relaxing on the beach in Thailand. We didn't know when we began our journey that we would experience major modifications to our well-thought-out plan.

Rochelle was exhausted on the flight to Atlanta, and we both were happy to arrive at my son's home where we could unwind and get a proper sleep. Proper sleep never happened. Rochelle's "hangover" from her tough workload didn't go away. She tossed and turned and required several pillows to prop her up in a comfortable enough position to nod off on occasion before awaking to more discomfort.

We did a bit of touring in Atlanta with my son, his wife, and their children, but Rochelle had a tough time keeping up whenever we had to walk. She was no more rested at the end of these few days than she was when we left the Middle East.

Upon arrival in Calgary, Rochelle and I, as often happened in the summer, were whisked off in different directions. My son was at the airport to greet me and take me to his home while Lori did the same, taking Rochelle to her home. This reduced our communication to daily phone calls. The one day when we did get together was to take my grandson to a movie, and Rochelle couldn't keep up on the walk through the mall to the theater and required several rest stops.

Back at her daughter's place, Rochelle's daughter became so concerned with her mother's appearance that she took Rochelle to the hospital emergency room.

The nurse took one look at Rochelle exclaiming, "Is she always this colour?" Rochelle was pushed to the front of the several-hour queue to a bed in the emergency ward. Medical staff performed immediate tests on Rochelle because of her artificial heart valve and related pacemaker. Blood tests revealed that Rochelle's hemoglobin count was a dangerous seventy-seven rather than the normal one hundred thirty. She appeared to be losing blood and was in congestive heart failure. Rochelle was immediately admitted to the hospital.

The beauty of the Canadian health-care system is that the first priority is the health of the patient rather than how the customer will pay, as is common in other jurisdictions. Money was never mentioned even though we could not produce an Alberta Health Care Insurance card. We showed them our medical insurance card from the UAE and nothing more was said.

Initial examination determined that Rochelle had blood in her stool that was originating either from her stomach or her bowels. She was bleeding to death and required transfusions to replace the lost blood. The transfusions brought her hemoglobin to an acceptable one hundred twenty. The next task was to ascertain from where the blood was originating.

The first procedure was an endoscopy to examine her stomach. When the doctors heard about our time in China, they suspected a bug that had been lying dormant for several years might be the culprit, causing bleeding ulcers. This theory proved negative, so the next step was a colonoscopy to see if the bleeding was originating from her bowels.

A colonoscopy requires complete eradication of everything from your bowels, so no food intake. In addition, Rochelle had to drink a chalky fluid to aid in the cleansing of her bowels—not a pleasant experience. Then she was given a drug to help her deal with the extreme discomfort of having a tube stuck up her rear. She was conscious during the procedure and experienced the discomfort in a haze, but she forgot most of it after its completion.

The procedure showed two polyps, one of which was four centimeters and had ruptured, causing the bleeding.

Normally, a doctor would remove the polyps during this procedure. However, Rochelle was taking blood thinners for her heart issues, and the doctor didn't want to risk further bleeding. At first, the doctor gave us the option of removing the polyps now or waiting until we returned to the UAE after they had brought her blood count to an acceptable level. We opted for the later procedure so we could salvage some of our holiday time.

However, continued excessive blood in Rochelle's stool removed the holiday option. The large polyp was still bleeding, and she would have bled to death before we finished our trip. So the doctor scheduled a second colonoscopy after they had sufficiently thickened her blood to avoid bleeding. This procedure was intended to allow the removal of the two polyps.

Now Rochelle had to go through a second uncomfortable round of cleansing her bowels and drinking the putrid brew provided by the pleasant, skilled, and helpful nurses. Another dose of the mind-numbing drug and she was taken away for the second probing of her bottom with the hopes of eliminating the source of her ailments.

Lori and I waited outside the operating room for Rochelle's emergence. Many other patients came and went, wheeled in and out of operating rooms with similar procedures but no sign of Rochelle. We began to worry and made nervous small talk to hide our fears.

Finally, after more than double the time of the routine procedure had elapsed, Rochelle was wheeled out in her bed. Although still groggy, she was visibly upset and very angry. The doctor told us that he had removed the smaller polyp but was unable to tackle the larger one due to its size and awkward location. He informed us that a specialist would have to remove the big polyp in a third procedure—thus Rochelle's anger at having to go through the detested routine again. In her delirium, she uttered unusually foul language and demanded an ambulance to take her away from all of this.

We had already used up nearly two weeks of our precious vacation time with no relaxation yet. Because of Rochelle's other issues, these normal procedures took much more time than would otherwise be expected because of having to thicken or thin out Rochelle's blood depending on what was being planned on any given day.

She was still receiving occasional transfusions to keep her blood count above the danger zone. In addition, she was getting several blood tests each day to monitor her blood thickness—thick for operating day and thin for recovery and eventual hospital discharge.

Next up, the third and, hopefully, last colonoscopy for the removal of the offending growth. A specialist from Toronto happened to be in town and was assigned the operation. This one went smoothly and quickly with the brash, self-assured, but obviously efficient doctor bragging to us about the procedure and how he had accomplished it. He even gave us a series of photographs of the polyp before and after and pointed out a "tattoo" he had placed at the site where the polyp used to be. It was only at this point that he asked about payment, as he was not part of the hospital billing system. He took a copy of our health insurance card from the UAE, and that was the last we heard about money.

Rochelle's bleeding problem was now history, and with some more transfusions her hemoglobin count was almost normal. Discharge from the hospital was now dependent on her blood thickness (INR), which had to be brought within an acceptable range. This magic number was reached within a couple of days, and we could now proceed with the rest of our holiday.

The Canadian health-care system was fast, courteous, and efficient. The hospital and the doctors billed our insurance company directly, so we didn't incur out-of-pocket expenses. The bill probably exceeded $50,000. Thank goodness we didn't go to a hospital in the United States.

Rochelle was discharged was Friday, July 2, and we had consumed almost three weeks of our summer holiday. We now planned to continue with our trip to Chicago and back to Atlanta. But we decided to cancel Thailand to allow Rochelle some recovery time back in Al Ain.

Rochelle was still very weak during our time in Chicago, where we had three events planned— Tony's vow renewal, his son's baptism, and my writing conference. The whole time Rochelle struggled to keep going, but we were able to accomplish all that we planned and even attended a couple of live theater performances. We hopped the plane for Atlanta where we still had a few days of visiting before returning home.

While Rochelle was sitting and catching her breath after the long walk to our gate at Midway Airport in Chicago, we both noticed a large swelling in her ankles. This was a sure sign that she was retaining fluid and might well be back in congestive heart failure. After arriving in Atlanta at my son's place, I made the decision to catch the next available flight back home to have Rochelle's health issue dealt with immediately. I didn't want to risk being caught in the black hole of the American health-care system, where green is the only colour that matters.

I had no trouble cancelling our Thailand trip for a full refund, and for a small change fee, Delta Airlines put us on the next direct flight to Dubai. We got home to Al Ain late at night, and the next morning went direct to Rochelle's heart doctor at American Hospital in Dubai. "American" is just the name; it actually has no affiliation with the United States in any manner. It is a luxury, private hospital that was connected to our health insurer for billing purposes.

Rochelle's doctor, whom she had just visited a month earlier and had given her a clean bill of health, rushed Rochelle into the emergency unit for testing and eventual admission to the hospital for further treatment.

The UAE health-care system is patterned after the US model with private hospitals and insurance. They will not proceed on most treatments without knowing where there money will come from. The biggest difference from the US model is that they seldom deny a claim. The hospital wanted to charge my credit card with a deposit, after receiving approval from the insurance company. I knew from our insurance provider previously that approval was usually immediate, so any delay was from the health provider not taking the time to ask the insurer. I stood my ground until they finally called the insurance company and got the necessary approval. After that, we were given excellent treatment with no mention of money.

Rochelle's major symptoms were shortness of breath and swelling in the abdomen and on the legs.

The first stop was the ICU (intensive care unit). Her heart doctor wanted to have her monitored continuously while diagnosing and treating her condition. She spent a couple of days in ICU, where she received diuretics to deal with the obvious fluid retention and an increased dosage of her blood thinner. She never achieved the optimum level of blood thickness after her procedure in Calgary.

Further testing showed that her pacemaker was working fine, but her heart was not able to work hard enough to expel the fluids from her body. So the doctor increased her heart rate on the pacemaker from sixty beats per minute to seventy beats per minute for the lower limit. That combined with the diuretic seemed to fix the fluid-retention problem. The only thing that concerned me about the increased heart rate was that the suggestion came from me. I had asked the doctor if that would help, and he did it. Why didn't he figure it out first?

As a precaution, Rochelle was fully examined for complications from her colon procedures in Calgary in addition to a check of her gall bladder. Everything else was fine.

She was then transferred to a regular ward unit (more about those facilities below) for a couple of days of monitoring. Her breathing returned to normal, and the fluid seemed to be completely gone. At that point she was just suffering from extreme fatigue and weakness from the ordeal of the past two months. Rochelle's tiny frame had lost over 15 percent of its mass and she was skin and bones. As some might say, she was "a pirates' dream—a sunken chest."

American Hospital in Dubai

This is a story in itself, especially contrasted with the hospital in Canada. Rochelle's stay and treatment was all covered by our insurance, but I would have to pay for any nights I stayed and any meals I consumed. This seemed fair.

Emergency ward

Rochelle received immediate and continuous care when admitted to the emergency ward. She had her own room, and for the longest time, she was the only patient in emergency. There was one doctor, an assistant or intern, a couple of nurses, some porters, and an administrator all dealing with her issues. Once they received the approval from our insurance carrier, they moved her to the ICU.

ICU (intensive care unit)

Once again, Rochelle had her own room with her own toilet for her two night stay. Not luxury accommodations but the room was better than many hotels I have stayed in. There was no extra bed, but there was a fancy recliner that I could rest and even sleep in. I spent one night there. The other night, I had to return to Al Ain to attend to personal affairs. The nurses don't work like they do in Canada, but then I don't think they have the capacity to do some of the intense work that the Canadian nurses have to do. Each nurse was assigned two rooms, which means two patients. They took care of regular monitoring and administration of medication, but other than that they were more like maids, fetching whatever you needed. They wouldn't let you do anything for yourself, including retrieving ice.

Regular ward

I wouldn't put it in the category of a five-star

hotel, but it was far superior to many three- and four-star hotels I have stayed in and was considerably more comfortable than the acceptable ICU. Rochelle had a regular hospital bed, but the rest of the room was more like a hotel. There was a large built-in sofa that I could use for sleeping. There was a built-in desk with Internet access, but I had to provide my own computer. We had a private toilet with shower and a large picture window overlooking a beautiful courtyard. The nurses were not overworked. We hardly ever saw a nurse, but they were available if you needed them—mainly for fetching pillows, blankets, etc. Rochelle was hooked up to a mobile monitoring device, so her readings were transmitted wirelessly and continuously. Other than daily blood work and administration of pills and injections, the nurses didn't have to do much. They certainly didn't have the patient load that a Canadian nurse would have, neither did it seem that they had the same competence, nice but dumb. Many of them spent their days playing games on the computers at their desks. Again, we were both served meals from the cafeteria after putting in our daily requests.

I don't know how to judge hospital equipment, but it appeared that the hospital had some of the best equipment that money could buy. It was always available, and it didn't seem to get much usage. Compare this to the hospital in Calgary that was always bustling. The Arab doctors seem to be very competent, helpful, and friendly. Although of Arabic background, they were all American trained and certified, with extensive experience in the United States.

The biggest problem for me was the daily drive when I didn't stay the night. It's a long drive from Al Ain to Dubai, and the road was under major construction.

Rochelle was finally discharged July 26, leaving only a couple of weeks of holiday time to recover before our final semester in Al Ain. The insurance covered the treatment and the bill for my extras amounted to the equivalent of about twenty-five Canadian dollars.

Here is Rochelle's summary of the ordeal, written immediately after her discharge:

Hello!
Yes, I'm still here!
As you all know last year was a stressful year for me. Once I took on the job as chair of the department (which I didn't want to do), I was determined to make a difference. I did get a lot accomplished and got lots of praise.
But *by the end of the year, I was totally exhausted...I could hardly wait to get to Lori's and just relax. Brian would stay with Cam's (his younger son's) family while Lori and I would take it easy.*
When I got to Lori's, she took one look at me and said I looked awful. I told her I just needed a few days and I would be fine.
Well, after a few days, I still had no energy, I wasn't sleeping, and I wasn't eating. Lori said, "We are going to emergency to get things checked out."
In emergency, they found my red blood cell (hemoglobin) count was seventy-seven (normal is over one hundred twenty) and I had fluid on my

lungs. The reason my blood count was so low was that I was hemorrhaging somewhere inside. They admitted me and it was decided they would look at my stomach (bleeding ulcer) and my colon (colonoscopy). I was given three pints of blood to perk me up and a strong diuretic to get rid of the fluid.

The endoscope (look at the stomach) found no trace of an ulcer. However, the colonoscopy uncovered two polyps, but because I am on blood thinner they were afraid to remove them until my blood was thicker.

The next day I underwent a second colonoscopy. Brian and Lori waited outside, as they had during the first one, I was not a happy camper. After ninety minutes, I was wheeled out, and we were told they only removed one of the polyps. The other was too difficult to remove in its current location, and they booked a third colonoscopy with a specialist for the next day.

Brian and Lori had their hands full, as I was extremely angry and was letting any doctor or nurse around know it.

The next day, the specialist was able to remove the large polyp, but as you can imagine I was totally exhausted. On top of already being run down, I had just gone through three colonoscopies and one endoscopy.

They kept me in the hospital to get my blood thin again and check fluid retention. Finally, after ten days they let me out.

But, *as you can imagine I was in not good shape. They had found why my red blood count was down, and why I was exhausted. They had fixed that but, I still had no energy, no stamina.*

And it was decision time;

We were to leave for Chicago and Brian's grandson's baptism and as well as a vow renewal for Tony and Lisa. Do I stay and rest at Lori's and have my heart checked to make sure it is OK. or do I go back home alone to Dubai and have my heart doctor check out things, or *do I go on to Chicago and take it easy until we get back to Dubai?*

Well, I decided to go on. I told Lori, Rob, and Brian that it was my choice. Maybe not the smartest choice but my choice. It was what I wanted to do.

So we went on to the family. I was not at my best and took things slow.

When we got back to the UAE, we immediately went to my heart doctor. He, of course, put me in the hospital in Dubai straight away and checked out my heart and pacemaker. They did some adjustment to the pacemaker to make it work harder, and I am going to be on diuretic pills for a while.

Now, it seems all I need is time to regain my strength.

Hopefully, within a month I will have my energy back and feel like my old self.

Hamad Heart Hospital

Another Middle Eastern country and another Middle Eastern hospital - September 2011

A hair-raising story in three parts:

Part 1—background and admission

We moved to Doha in January 2011, and by spring Rochelle had located the only pacemaker clinic in the city at Hamad Hospital, a government-run institution among a plethora of private hospitals all within walking distance of one another.

At her June appointment, Doctor Saeed at the pacemaker clinic reported that there was still eighteen to thirty months left on her current pacemaker, which had been installed in Calgary about ten years earlier; it had served her well. He said, however, that she should come back right after our summer vacation to have it checked again, and he would keep monitoring it every month thereafter. Her first trip back in September showed a reading of "ERI," or elective replacement indicated. This message had replaced the normal message giving the number of months remaining in the life of the device. ERI is one step before the message "EOL," meaning end of life. I'm not sure if that means end of the life of the unit or the end of the patient's life. Regardless, Doctor Saeed said it was time to get a new unit—and soon.

What followed was a series of appointments and tests at the pacemaker clinic and the Hamad cardiology unit. Up to this time, I had not been directly involved as Rochelle's appointments were always during my working hours. Rochelle always came back from these appointments frustrated, confused, and in a tizzy. It sounded like disorganized chaos at the hospital. So I tried to get her to schedule appointments when I could come along and get the information first-hand.

My first visit showed my some of the reasons for Rochelle's state of mind. First of all, Rochelle went into full panic mode even before reaching the hospital. Her normal calm, mature demeanour disappeared, and she became a blithering fool, unable to form full sentences and communicate a coherent message. The other reason I found out was that the hospital (and hospitals in general in Doha) are staffed with very nice and polite Middle Easterners and Asians who would have trouble understanding how to perform the duties of a Walmart greeter, let alone how to run a hospital. This definitely applied to all administrators, and for the most part the well-intentioned nursing staff. We did find a reasonable level of competence with the actual medical staff, especially the doctors.

We were greeted by these "nice" people who immediately asked to see Rochelle's appointment card. This would be the start of setting Rochelle off because she was never given an appointment card. Doctor Saeed always had her phone his mobile as soon as she arrived at the clinic and he or someone would come and fetch her. It seemed like the medial staff didn't really want to rely on the administration, so they always had a "back-door" way of doing things.

After a series of fits and false starts, cancelled appointments, and other emergencies by the doctors, she was given an admission date—Tuesday, October 4. We arranged to go together right after work and get her admitted to the brand new Hamad Heart Hospital, a separate facility from the main hospital. So new, in fact, that the pacemaker clinic had not yet relocated.

As we entered the lobby, we were greeted by a well-dressed gentleman in a dark suit who welcomed us to the hospital and asked how he could help. I told him that my wife was being admitted for a pacemaker replacement. He asked for our admitting card, which, of course, we did not have. He then took us to a Qatari gentleman, dressed in his white thobe, who was the head of admitting. While I was dealing with these two gentlemen, Rochelle got on her mobile phone to Doctor Saeed. The whole lobby reeked of confusion and chaos. I was trying to explain to these two administrators that we were not issued an admitting card and that we always just called the doctor. Then Doctor Kassim, one of the heart doctors showed up. He exchanged a few heated words with the administrators in Arabic, and the only word I picked up was "emergency." Again, it was clear that Rochelle's doctors had their own plan for admission that didn't involve the front door.

Doctor Kassim whisked us away to the emergency ward where Rochelle was beset upon by at least a half a dozen nurses, who were all referred to as "sister." My immediate thoughts were that Larry, Curly, and Moe had a bunch of daughters and they all ended up as "sisters" at the Hamad Heart Hospital. These Asian (Filipina and Indian) ladies were tripping over each other to deal with Rochelle's "emergency."

They stripped Rochelle down, slipped a gown on her, put her in an emergency bed, strapped her up to every imaginable wire and gadget, and began firing questions at her. "How do you feel? Do you have any pain? Is your chest tight?" They started filling out forms and each nurse took a turn asking the same questions over and over again in broken English. Each of them wrote the answers on their form, but no one ever seemed to read the previous reports because this became a standard procedure for the rest of Rochelle's time in the hospital. She was repeatedly asked the same questions: "How long have you had this pacemaker? Do you feel dizzy? Are you on medication?"

Rochelle was the only patient in the emergency ward and had the full attention of every one of the plentiful staff who seemed to be just waiting for some emergency to beset them. Doctor Kassim had disappeared, and we were now left to the mercy of the daughters of Larry, Curly, and Moe. Before he disappeared, the doctor had assured us that Rochelle was scheduled for 8:00 a.m. the next morning to have her pacemaker replaced.

The emergency room doctor showed up and began to ask all the same questions that had been written on all the previous forms that he had never read. We were told that Rochelle would be sent to her room shortly because they had a quality standard of no more than a one-hour stay in the emergency ward.

The daughters of the Stooges then abandoned us to visit and giggle around the nursing station desks with a large dark-skinned gentleman in hospital garb, who resembled a character from a gangster movie. Other than the occasional visit from one of the mauve clad sisters, we were left alone to wait and wait. The one-hour quality standard had been exceeded considerably. I went to ask one of the nurses who was at the desk, and she said that the doctor had to sign the admission form.

I asked, "When would that be?"

She replied, "We don't know. We can't find him right now. He must be busy."

After another fifteen minutes, I asked the "gangster" guy when we would be going to a room, and he got on the phone right away. After about two and a half hours in the emergency, we were finally on our way to the wards to see more daughters of the Stooges in action. The next part of the story comes from the horse's mouth—the patient herself.

Part 2—the operation—in the words of the patient, who was awake during the whole procedure.

Doctor Kassim, who admitted me and who has been involved since early on in the planning, came to see me on Tuesday evening to check on how I was doing and to give me the plan for the next morning—operation day. He assured me that I was going in at 8:00 a.m. the next morning. He also promised that he would come and see me the morning prior to the operation, telling the nurse to make sure I was ready to go for 8:00 a.m. He and Doctor Saeed (the pacemaker tech, maybe not even a doctor) were the only ones to instill any confidence that my operation could be successfully performed here.

True to his word, Doctor Kassim showed up at 7:00 a.m. Wednesday morning to tell me that everything was set for 8:00 a.m. and to re-inform the nurse to have me in the operating room at 8:00 a.m. Shortly before 8:00 a.m., I saw an orderly bring the transport bed and park it outside my room. Then I waited and waited. Finally, at 8:45 a.m. my nurse came in and started to get me ready to go to the operating room and wheeled me down in time for a 9:00 a.m. start.

I was wheeled into a little "holding" room where I was told to wait. Based on my experience to date, I wasn't confident that anyone would even remember where they left me.

As I lay there, I heard Doctor Kassim start shouting at my nurse, "I told you 8:00 a.m. I put it on the chart, 8:00 a.m. I reminded you this morning that it was 8:00 a.m. Look at the time. It's now 9:00 a.m. We are an hour behind, and we have two more procedures after this one. We almost had to cancel." He continued to berate and chastise the negligent nurse for several minutes, and I don't know to what end. The damage had already been done, and it was time to get to work. I was in fear that my procedure would be cancelled, and I didn't want to have to go through this chaos again.

Temped to jump out of bed and bolt for the door, I shouted out, "Hello. I'm in here. Are we ready to start soon?" After about ten minutes, they moved me into the operating room—over an hour behind schedule.

I was surrounded by five nurses, all busy doing nothing productive and arguing about whose job was what. Doctor Kassim and Doctor Saeed were both present in addition to a heart surgeon plus a couple other assorted males, bringing my entourage to about ten people.

Everyone seemed to have a task: setting up monitors or IVs, setting up the operating table, and prepping me for the upcoming procedure. It was chaos with lots of fussing and arguing. Next, the nurses started to fiddle with my clothes and bedding and then one of them shouted, "OK, all the men out, now." One of the few times the nurses had any ability to tell the doctors what to do. The males all dutifully exited the room while the females, all Indian nurses, continued to fuss over my "appearance." It was their job to make sure that I was appropriately covered in all the right places, so none of the men could get corrupted by a glimpse of any of my personal parts. When all the modesty coverings were in place, the men were summoned back to the operating room. Thank goodness there had been no emergency in the meantime; these nurses were obviously trained at the "Larry, Curly, and Moe Academy of Nursing." They instilled no confidence whatsoever.

Upon re-entry to the operating room, Doctor Saeed looked at the scene and blew a gasket.

"I told you her pacemaker is on her right-hand side. You have set up the whole procedure on her left. Get that fixed and now." The nurses hopped at the order and moved all the paraphernalia to the other side of the operating table. Again, the door looked very tempting—maybe I could catch a 10:00 a.m. plane to Sanityville. Doctor Saeed could see I was agitated and restless. Big deal; it's only my life at stake. He tried to calm me and said that everything was under control.

Now Doctor Kassim took charge of the task of hooking me up to a temporary external pacemaker. Being 100 percent reliant on the pacemaker in my chest, I couldn't afford to be without an electrical impulse to my heart for even one minute. I knew they talked about a temporary pacemaker, but I wasn't really clear on how they would do this. Nothing so far resembled my previous procedures years ago in Canada.

Doctor Kassim took a scalpel and sliced into my inner right thigh. I could see on the monitor as he pushed a wire through my vein to my heart.

"A little to the left. No, right. OK. Looks good," someone barked as Doctor Kassim pushed.

"Now, let's see if this works," Doctor Kassim proclaimed. I wished he would keep his commentary to himself. What if it didn't work? What was the back-up plan then? Then cheers erupted as he flipped the switch and the beeper started to go, and the waves appeared on the screen. This was supposed to be a standard procedure, not a shuttle launch. Being hooked to the machine as I was now removed any further temptation to run for the door, which still looked appealing given the gong show I was experiencing. I had flashbacks to my ordeals in Cyprus, London, and Karachi and thought how this made those experiences pale by comparison. I was in fear for my life as Doctor Kassim gave the signal to the heart doctor to disconnect my current pacemaker that had kept me alive for the past ten years. Again, more faint cheers from the crowd as I had survived another milestone, still alive.

The heart doctor, who never did reveal his identity probably for security reasons in case I expired, then started to cut into my chest to start the process of removing the old unit.

"Scalpel," he demanded of the nearest nurse. "Scissors," he continued. "Screwdriver." Wait! Did he say screwdriver? What the hell does he need with a screwdriver? Are a tire iron and hammer next?

He dug and gouged for what seemed like an hour. I was pushed and pulled in every direction as he tried to extract this piece of metal that had actually become a part of my body. I don't ride roller coasters, but I'm sure this was a worse ride. Then it popped out and he held up the bloody, tissue encrusted plate and showed it to me.

"See, this is what was inside you," he announced with a certain degree of pride.

I don't know why, but I instinctively replied, "Can I keep it?"

"Sure," he said as he passed the contraption to a nurse to clean it up for me.

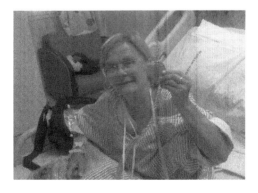

Now for the new, modern smaller model to take the place of the old clunker. Doctor Heart again started to prod and push, exclaiming that he couldn't make it fit. Why can't these guys keep their mouths shut when they are doing this?

"Maybe if you turn it this way," said one of the extra doctors.

"Put it in the other way," offered another. More confidence-building commentary making me wish that I had just let the old one run its course.

But eventually he got it in and turned on, and they disconnected the temporary external machine, and I was still breathing. The worst was now over.

"Pass me the glue," he continued and proceeded to "glue" my incision shut, fanning it dry with a piece of paper.

They wheeled me into the "holding" room and said my nurse would come to get me. I've seen this movie before. I wasn't about to be left stranded and abandoned in some holding tank.

"My husband is waiting for me," I barked. "I need to get to my room now." I asserted my authority.

"She will be here in a minute," the attending nurse informed me.

"No," I insisted. "Call her now. I can't wait here." Shortly, my nurse did show up and wheeled me back to my room where Brian had been pacing for four hours with no word about my ordeal. But it was over and now just the healing remained.

Part 3—the discharge—by Brian

Originally scheduled for Thursday, the day after the operation, Rochelle's discharge was delayed because we were waiting for her blood to reach the right level of thickness. She takes warfarin to thin her blood because of her artificial valve. Other than the occasional follow-up visit from the doctor, all she could do was wait until they said she was ready. That gave her lots of time to observe and be entertained by the comedy act that passed for hospital procedures. Fortunately, she had a private room, so she could close her door as needed. Much of the time she was hooked up to IV that pumped blood thinner into her system, thus restricting her freedom of movement.

The ward was full. Every room had someone in it, and there was an overabundance of nurses except when they were needed or wanted. The call buzzers were going constantly as were the phones at the nurses' stations. All of which went unanswered all the time. Doctors even complained to the nurses, "Don't you ever answer the phones?" Not when there is visiting to do or a coffee break or meal time. There were times when half a dozen of the "sisters" could be seen hanging around the nursing station while buzzers and phones were polluting with air with unnecessary sound. Other times, you could walk the length of the ward and never see a nurse. When they were around, they had a standard set of answers for all questions that were designed to get the patients off their backs. Patients were such a nuisance.

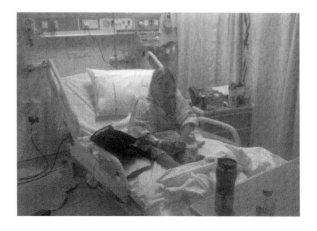

Friday morning, the doctor gave the word that Rochelle could go home; all was well. Now how long to get out of this den of comedy? Rochelle and I sat and waited for something to happen to let us know we could leave. Rochelle decided to get dressed to try to speed things up, but she needed to get all the contraptions removed from her body.

When she asked the nurse to do this, the nurse said, "Just a minute," and then disappeared faster than a Carrefour "may-I-help-you" worker (that's another Middle Eastern service story). Finally, all the prods and probes were removed, and we waited some more.

"What's the hold up now?"

"The doctor must sign the forms."

"Call the doctor."

"We don't know where he is."

The nurses have minimal training, low motivation, and absolutely no authority. They are constantly berated by their Arab patients and the superior doctors, so they are motivated to just stay out of the way and not be seen. They do this very well.

But they definitely don't want to overstep their bounds and get in trouble with anyone who might be their superior—which is actually everyone.

I saw this as an opportunity to speed things up and told the nurse, "We're leaving now. I'll give you my number, and you can call us when the doctor shows up." This announcement horrified the nurse, who got on the phone right away and tracked down the doctor. She didn't want to be responsible for an escaped patient.

Finally, we were on our way home for healing and recovery. We tried to keep ourselves healthy and fit for the rest of our time in Doha. This was not the place you wanted to be sick and in hospital.

My Kingdom for a Horse

Egyptian Adventure
January 2005

There is no place for a pedestrian to cross the busy streets, and the traffic lights are purely decoration. Red or green lights do not seem to affect the traffic flow. To cross the street, you close your eyes and start walking into the traffic and somehow you miraculously arrive on the other side. In spite of the wall-to-wall cars and no adherence to lanes (two lanes accommodate five cars abreast), traffic seems to move. Thus is traffic in Cairo.

All local residents are well trained in how to fleece the tourists.

My son Cam and I had just checked into our hotel right on the Nile River when we went for a walk and encountered a fourteen-year-old boy who was quite friendly. He tried to have us come to his "gallery" to see his artwork. With considerable effort, we were finally able to shake him. Many other local residents tried to do the same, but we were able to avoid them.

The next morning, we decided to walk to the Egyptian Museum. We were staying near the museum. Again, we encountered a local resident who was walking along and immediately became our friend. He wanted to tell us about his country—no charge, as usual. We found ourselves being guided down some back streets to a local shop where a friend of his was prepared to give us discounted tours of the pyramids. Again with some effort, we were able to escape this attempt at unlicensed tourism.

We decided to do our own touring without the aid of a tour guide. I used my limited Arabic to negotiate a good price with a taxi driver to take us to the pyramids which weren't far from our hotel. All seemed to be going very well as we approached the ancient structures.

Then the taxi slowed to a crawl, and a middle-aged stout gentleman jumped in the front seat of the cab and said hello to me in Arabic. I recognized the words and responded with the appropriate Arabic reply. However, he did speak very good English and said he was just catching a ride to his home and if we were uncomfortable he would leave. I said he could stay, and that gave him the opportunity to tell us how to see the pyramids the Egyptian way, by camel or horseback, our choice.

I wasn't too keen on this, sensing another heavy come-on, but our conversation continued. Soon we came to a stop on a side road in a poor district of Giza, not far from the pyramids. We were then invited into a local home for some tea and more pressure to take an Egyptian tour. The prices quoted were considerably more than we could get through hotel tour desk, so I said thank you and started to leave.

Then our newly minted tour guide said, "What price would you like?" I responded with a ridiculously low price to shake him off, but he accepted my number.

Next thing we knew, we were on horses and heading down some back roads in the slums of Giza with our guide sitting on a horse at the rear of our trio, with me in the lead followed by Cam. After a few minutes of riding alongside the large fence that keeps people from the pyramid lands, we came to a hole in the fence guarded by some local residents and we were through the fence, horses and all, with no entry fees. We spent the next hour riding our horses around next to the pyramids. We rode right up to one of the pyramids and had a great time exploring.

I had not ridden a horse since childhood, but my limited skills came back to me. No one told me what I could or couldn't do with the horse, nor did anyone tell the horse what he could do with me. The horse tried several times to reach around and bite my leg, but I was able to show him who was boss. However, as we approached the Sphinx, the horse couldn't resist the clean, white sand and decided to go for a roll. He dropped to his knees and started to roll over onto his side. I was able to get out of his way before he rolled on top of me. Between our guide and me we were able to get the horse back on his feet, and I got back on, now firmly in charge and taking no guff from the beast, who could have caused me considerable damage.

It was a great trip, and I would do it again. It was well worth the low price we paid, which, of course, included a generous tip to cover the bribes our guide had to fork out to various "guards" along our route. It was definitely not a pyramid visit that most tourists would ever experience.

That afternoon, we finally did walk over to the museum and got to see all of the ancient treasures and mummies. Again, we had to fight off tour guides who were willing to show us the real Cairo and the museum.

By this time, we decided that our best bet was to use the hotel services and take properly licenced tours. Our first trip was to Sacarra and Memphis, which are close to Cairo and the sites of the very first pyramids ever built. For some reason, we seemed to be between major tourist times so on each of our tours, there was just Cam, me, the tour guide, and the bus driver.

That night, we took in the sound and light show at the pyramids and the Sphinx. This was a laser-light show that gave a good historical account of the location. The next day, we took a day drip to the pyramids and Sphinx and saw it all again the normal tourist way.

One night, we took a trip to the largest souk (market) where every vendor tried to hook the only tourists in sight—us. It seemed that most of the shoppers were locals and the tourists were rare. Again, quite the experience. At the time, Cairo was a very safe place for tourists, but only a week after our trip, a bomb was set off in the very souk that Cam and I had walked through.

Our final adventure was the trip to the airport. We were running late, and our driver was faced with major traffic problems as we weaved through the many artificial lanes. Somehow, we did arrive on time and after fighting through unorganized and slow lines at the inefficient and dirty airport, we were finally on our way back to Dubai.

Arctic Adventures

I spent four years living in Canada's Arctic with my first wife, Marlene. Here are a couple of my more noteworthy experiences.

Do You Feel a Pang?
March 1995

Pangurtung, in the middle of Baffin Island, was always one of my favourite destinations with its tall, mountainous terrain bordering on a fjord leading to the frozen salt water of Cumberland Sound. In spite of the minus thirty degree Celsius temperatures outside, I had a warm feeling knowing that the two-and-a-half-hour roller coaster flight was about to come to an end.

The faces of the three fellow passengers that I could see showed even more distress than I felt as the pilot had battled incredible headwinds in a winter blizzard that would have kept most planes grounded and should have kept ours grounded at our point of embarkation, Iqaluit. Three additional passengers were hidden from my sight due to their obscure seating positions in the seven-seater, single-engine aircraft. One was in the co-pilot seat next to our young pilot and the other, a young Inuit woman with a newborn baby in her arms, was tucked in the tail section of the crowded craft. The poor woman, just beyond childhood herself, was still stressed from her childbirth ordeal in the capital "city" of Iqaluit; the buffeting flight didn't ease her distress as she had sobbed the entire flight. Other than the Inuit woman and her baby, we were all white southerners. In the Arctic, anyone living below the Arctic Circle is considered a southerner.

My new-found relief gave way to escalating stress when a few hundred meters above the short gravel runway, the pilot pulled the nose up and gunned the already strained engine of the small craft. Even though my seat faced backwards, the eyes in the back of my head told me that we were approaching the sheer mountain that I knew from previous landings draped the far end of the runway. The plane raced for the sky clearing the precipice that could have become our final resting place. Now what?

I wasn't even supposed to be on this flight. The airline that I booked my flight from Iqaluit to Pangurtung with had cancelled their sole weekly flight—probably because I was the only passenger listed. So I scrambled to find an alternative. I got the last seat on this little plane. I sat knee to knee facing a large middle-aged white woman. Beside her sat a nondescript gentleman, who sat knee to knee with the male passenger to my left. Our baggage was crammed into the tail section, behind the young Inuit mother, held in place with mesh straps.

The sky could not have been darker when we took off from the nearly three-kilometer-long Iqaluit airstrip in heavy winds and blowing snow. We took off into the wind and battled a strong headwind all the way to Pangurtung. The plane was tossed back and forth and up and down. The pilot did his best to keep the plane steady while everyone on board had a green tinge to their faces in the dim light of the cramped plane. The poor Inuit woman in the back was whimpering to herself while her baby slept in her arms.

Our momentary relief at the impending landing in Pang (the common nickname for the tiny Inuit village) turned to gasping panic as the plane raced for the sky. The pilot never said a word as it became clear we were not going to land, and the plane appeared to turn back toward our origin. The strong headwind on our trip to Pang was now a gale-force tailwind, making the first leg of the trip seem wonderful by comparison. I felt like the plane was going to tumble at any moment. The pilot had his hands glued to the controls trying to keep the plane under some form of control as our ground speed nearly matched the wind speed, making our air speed next to zero—a tough challenge for any pilot.

The pilot's silence was eerie, and it was clear all was not well.

The stout lady across from me leaned over and asked, "Can I hold your hand—I'm so scared." Grabbing her hand, I was petrified as well but didn't want to panic the others by demonstrating it. I was trying to remember where the pilot said the survival gear was stowed.

The fellow next to me seemed to be in the same state. We were complete strangers, but we both seemed to sense that we needed to keep everyone from thinking and talking about our dire situation. He and I struck up a light conversation, taking turns making inconsequential statements and cracking the odd funny. It seemed to keep the tension down, but everyone still had deep concern written on their faces. I felt like I could toss my cookies at any time. The Inuit woman continued sobbing with the quiet baby in her arms.

The trip back to Iqaluit seemed to take forever. Every bump and twist felt like it would be our last before plowing into the frozen mountains of Baffin Island. I could feel the plane descending. Was this Iqaluit or our frozen grave? Then I saw the lights of the runway. With the wind at our back, the pilot didn't even come around to land into the wind. He took full advantage of the long Iqaluit runway and landed with the wind behind him.

As the pilot brought the plane to a controlled stop, he sighed broke his long silence, "In seven years of flying, I have never flown in conditions like that. They should never have let us take off." When he got us safely into the Iqaluit terminal, he stormed off to give someone a piece of his mind. He told us that wind conditions in Pangurtung kept us from landing, but I later found out that there was actually some mechanical problem with the flaps that would have seen us crashing into the mountain if he hadn't aborted the landing.

In spite of the hair-raising flight, I was on another flight to Pangurtung the next day to fulfill my work obligations. It was a different plane and a different pilot and the daytime flying conditions were ideal—clear skies and no wind. Snow and ice blanketed the beauty of the picturesque Arctic Island as I gazed out the window.

With only me on this flight, the pilot turned around and spoke, "I'm new to Arctic flying. Would you mind if I just toured around a bit to see some of the sights?" I had no time commitments—you never do when you are on Inuit time.

I replied, "No problem. Take your time."

I continued to gaze at the wonder below me, having forgotten about the previous night's terror. As I soaked in the view, it occurred to me that people spent thousands of dollars to get an experience like this—and I was being paid.

Our landing in Pang was without incident, and the pilot jumped out of the door by his seat. I stood hunched over in the short craft as I shuffled to the passenger door near the back. As I looked out the window, I could see a truck which appeared to be moving toward the wing of the plane. On closer inspection I saw that there was no driver in the truck, which was actually stationary. It was the plane that was moving.

The pilot had forgotten to lock the wheels, and the plane was rolling backward down a slight slope on the gravel tarmac with me as the only occupant of the errant plane. I noticed people scrambling outside in a vain attempt to prevent the impending collision but to no avail. The wing of the plane struck the truck, resulting in a jolt that almost put me on the floor of the plane. With the plane now stationary, someone opened the passenger door and let me out. The pilot surveyed the damage to the plane's wing which now had a large dent in the flap. Obviously not interested in waiting in Pang the several days it might take for an engineer to come and fix the wing, the pilot used the brute force of his hands to bend the flap back into a position similar to its natural state. After my bag was tossed from the plane, the pilot got back behind the controls and took off back to Iqaluit.

A week later, I was ready for my return trip, and who should show up to take me back but the same pilot with the same plane, still with the visible dent in the flap. We returned without incident, proving to me once again that Arctic flying has a different set of rules.

Pulling Rankin
April 1996

The stamp on my boarding pass read, "We are not responsible for any delays due to weather"—a standard warning for air travel in Canada's Arctic. Weather was so unpredictable that you never knew if you would reach your proper destination or if you would be able to get out once you got there.

Weather conditions at departure in Yellowknife were good, but at Rankin Inlet, on the shores of Hudson Bay, they were not. Rankin was experiencing one of its common spring storms.

I was bundled up in my Snow Goose parka and Sorel mukluks, ready for the minus thirty degrees that awaited me in Rankin.

As the First Air Boeing 737 circled over the Inuit community looking for an opportunity to land in the heavy winds, the pilot announced, "We are unable to land in Rankin and are heading for our alternate destination—Winnipeg." I was never sure why Winnipeg was the alternate destination as it was over three hundred kilometers farther than just returning to Yellowknife.

When we landed in Winnipeg, the spring temperature was a balmy twenty-five degrees Celsius. My winter attire drew a plethora of stares from the local population. I could have been mistaken for an American coming to Canada for summer ski season. But it was easier to wear my Arctic gear than to carry it.

As per the airline's warning, I was on my own for transportation and accommodation until our next attempt the following day. So I called up my sister-in-law, Connie, and took a cab to her place where we had a great visit. I made a successful trip to Rankin Inlet the next day.

Endless Summer Sun, No Winter Fun

Fort McPherson August 1994

The sweat flowed from my brow as the low-hung sun beat on my hat and shirt as I jogged along the dusty gravel road. With a temperature of plus thirty-five degrees Celsius, it was no wonder that I was hot on a mid-August day. I delayed my run as late in the day as possible to take advantage of whatever relief from the heat the evening provided. But the sun had no intention of taking a rest; it would be up all night. This was summer in the Arctic in the Gwich'in community of Fort McPherson, a two-hour drive along the dusty Dempster Highway from the Inuvialuit community of Inuvik. In the summer, the sun never sets. It just circles the sky, baking the ground without relief. Summer temperatures near forty degrees Celsius were not uncommon in this part of the Arctic.

Baker Lake
June 1996

The sun was low on the horizon with no intention of dipping further. Its weak rays provided some warmth as it beat on the back of my parka while the spray from the surface water flew by me. I straddled the passenger position of the snowmobile as the driver scooted across the frozen lake. It was June 21—the longest day of the year. It was midnight, and I was on the surface of the lake that serves as Canada's geographic epicentre.

The irony of my situation hit me—midnight in the summer with the sun shining while riding on a snowmobile in the middle of a lake. How do you explain that to people who have never been to the Arctic?

The surface of the lake contained puddles of water created by the sun melting the ice. I worried about our safety, being in the middle of the lake on a land conveyance. However, a quick visit with some

Inuit fishermen proved the ice was still well over three feet thick, based on the hole from which they extracted their catch.

Life in the Arctic continued to provide me with a lifetime of memories.

Dark Days - January 1995

The sun doesn't rise in Yellowknife until after 10:00 a.m. in mid-winter. With only five hours of daylight, it is gone by 3:00 p.m. Thus, our boarding time of 9:00 a.m. on the First Air flight for Iqaluit saw us entering the plane as if it were the middle of the night.

My wife, Marlene, was accompanying me on one of my frequent business trips where I would spend one day in Iqaluit, on the southern end of Baffin Island, and then ten days in Pangurtung located in the central part of the same island. Iqaluit was our final destination for the day, but we had to take a circuitous route by way of Resolute Bay on Cornwallis Island in the Arctic Ocean. We planned to conclude our trip with a few days of holidays in Regina, which required a flight back to Iqaluit then another to Montreal before our final leg to Regina and then our return trip to Yellowknife.

The two-hour-plus flight and a time change put us in the small Arctic community of Resolute Bay around noon. There was no sunrise in the high Arctic in mid-winter, so there was nothing to greet us but the same darkness we encountered upon departure from Yellowknife.

Iqaluit is below the Arctic Circle. So even in the dead of winter, it sees a couple hours of dim daylight, but these hours had passed before our three-hour flight landed in the future capital of Nunavut. Thus, we arrived in the dark after 3:00 p.m., never having seen a ray of sunshine our entire trip—a whole day of darkness.

During our one day in Iqaluit, we took full advantage of the short daytime hours wandering the town in our full winter gear talking to carvers as they crafted their masterpieces.

Then we flew to Pangurtung without incident, unlike some of my other flights to the Inuit community. Pang, located much further north than Iqaluit, had a shorter span of daylight where the sun would break the horizon for several minutes before being pulled back down, casting dusk then darkness over the nine hundred mostly Inuit residents. After dropping us off, our plane made a scheduled trip to Broughton Island on the east coast of Baffin Island on Davis Strait before returning to Pang and then back to Iqaluit.

On our return trip, we arrived at the small airstrip just as the plane taking us back to Iqaluit was to land in Pang before its short journey across the island. I wanted to ask the pilot if he would let me and my wife sit on the flight to Broughton to see another part of the Arctic countryside – a free tour if you will.

His first response to me was a question, "Are you RCMP?"

To which I replied, "No." He welcomed us on board for the free flight to see another Inuit community. Where else can you take a free trip just for the asking?

We took a short walk around Broughton before the plane returned to Pang, then to Iqaluit, and then onto a larger plane for our journey to Montreal, our connection point for a family trip to Regina. Montreal winters do not resemble Arctic winters, so the Marlene and I were quite the spectacle as we walked from our arrival gate toward our next departure gate in full Arctic regalia—Snow Goose parkas and Sorrel mukluks.

We had a full set of stories to share on our visit to Regina.

And Now the Rest of the Story

The following stories fit the subject of travel, but do not neatly fit neatly into any of the previous categories.

They are cute, but not as exciting as the previous events. You may even have similar travel experiences.

Any stories that do not contain me directly involve my close family.

Lusting in Paris
July 2000

We had only been a couple for less than six months. Rochelle had just moved in to the apartment I shared with my adult son, and then immediately left for a six-week trip to Europe with her grown children.

Six weeks was too long to wait to see each other again, so we agreed that we would meet for a week in Paris during the middle of her holiday.

Rochelle met me in Terminal 10 at Charles de Gaulle Airport. She braved the Paris Métro on her own to make sure she was with me as soon as I got off the plane.

We talked on the phone often but had not seen each other for three weeks. Hungry for each other, we caught the first métro we could, rushing to our hotel in Pigalle—the Parisian sex district. The elevator was not big enough for Rochelle, me, and the luggage, so I sent her and the bags in the tiny cage while I ran up the four flights of stairs. I was so eager to be with her. I beat the elevator to the top.

We rushed into the room. No time for unpacking. Clothes flew in every direction. We were both looking for what we were missing for weeks.

Both fully satisfied and exhausted, we fell asleep in each other's arms—naked on the top of the bed.

When we awoke two hours later, we saw that in our haste we had neglected to close our door. From the old hallway, you could look right in our door to where we lay—still naked.

***

Parlez-Vous Français?
July 2000

Our week in Paris was now over, and it was time to say goodbye.

My flight from Paris to Calgary was delayed by several hours. Rochelle had accompanied me to the airport since she had time before she was to meet her son, Rob, at the train station for their trip to Spain. So, I decided to travel with her on the métro to see her off at the train.

After she and Rob departed, I decided to kill some more time by walking for a while before catching the métro back to de Gaulle Airport.

While walking, a young, attractive, Asian woman approached me. She spoke in very broken French "Où est le…Latin Quartier?"

Being a foreigner in Paris and not proficient in French myself, I was of little help, but I tried. "peut-etre la…" as I pointed to where I thought the district was located.

She tried a few more questions in French, and I tried in vain some weak French responses. We were both getting very frustrated with our inability to communicate.

Finally, she threw up her hands, "Do you speak any English at all?" she said in perfect Canadian English.

"Yes I do. I'm Canadian," I replied.

"Thank goodness," she sighed, "I'm Canadian too."

We both laughed and completed our conversation before parting ways.

Customers Are Such a Nuisance
July 2012

Air Canada: "We're not satisfied until you're not satisfied!" This is a quote from Craig Heisinger, Assistant General Manager of the Winnipeg Jets Hockey Club. We got a full taste of this tongue-in-cheek motto on our trip from Winnipeg to Calgary on July 30, 2012.

Rochelle and I arrived early at James Armstrong Richardson International Airport in Winnipeg and checked in with enough time to make sure we still had our previously selected seats and to have a leisurely breakfast before departure. This leg of our trip was booked along with our entire summer trip several months prior.

While sitting waiting for our "on-time" departure, with no plane at the gate, it became clear that we would not be departing on time. In fact, the plane ended up being over an hour late.

After an eternity of no communication, the gate attendant announced that there had been an equipment change. The plane we were using would be smaller, and they needed six volunteers to take a later flight because there weren't enough seats on the replacement plane. Almost immediately a couple of people took them up on the offer, and then shortly another couple did the same. Given that we had car and apartment booked at our destination city of Calgary, we did not want to take the later flight and wait around the Winnipeg airport with nothing to do.

The agent announced that they needed two more volunteers, and we saw no one approach the desk. Within a few minutes, they called my name and told me they were bumping us off this flight. I explained that we had this trip booked for months, they told us, "Too bad. We need to move you to the next flight." There was no more room for discussion or objection. They offered us travel vouchers in compensation. I told them that these didn't do us much good as we lived on the other side of the world. So, they offered us $100 cheques. Again, I informed them that a Canadian cheque did me little good as I live halfway around the world, and the fees to deposit the cheque would gobble up the face value. I asked if the vouchers were transferable, and they said that I could, but I had to be there to make the booking for whomever I was transferring the vouchers to. Again, I had to remind them that I lived far, far away in another land, and I couldn't travel back to make a booking for someone. I guess it takes repeating something several times to get it through or perhaps sound just travels so slow that they hadn't heard it the first time.

Finally, they agreed that we could transfer the voucher by way of signed letter, and we took that option, angry at their lack of concern and minimal customer service. They then booked us on the next flight, which required a three-hour wait in the airport. I asked if they would give us food vouchers while we waited, and they said yes. It turned out these food vouchers were for $10 each, which barely covered a ham sandwich and a bottle of water. Our modest breakfast had cost us $30 at the airport.

So we used up our vouchers and sat and read for the time it took to get on our later plane, which was also almost an hour late in departing. Upon arrival in Calgary, we waited for our luggage, but everyone walked away from the carousel with bags except us. I went to the Air Canada baggage counter where the lineup was so long for lost luggage that I wondered if we would ever get out of the airport.

When I looked out from the baggage office, I saw our bags sitting in the middle of the floor, nowhere near the luggage belt. They had obviously come on our original plane, and they neglected to tell us. Why would they? It would spoil their service record.

This put us in Calgary traffic during rush hour, and we missed the office closing time for our car rental and the apartment office hours, forcing us to use alternate methods of arranging our car and accommodation.

But we finally did get a car and get into our apartment, and all was well after a totally wasted day—one that we can never recapture.

Air Canada: "We're not satisfied until you're not satisfied!"

The Lost Boys
August 1995

The trip itinerary was complex. I would fly from Yellowknife to Toronto. My son, Cam, would fly standby from Regina to hopefully arrive in Toronto at about the same time as I landed. Marlene would fly from Yellowknife to Regina. Cam and I would drive from Toronto to Erie, Pennsylvania to see my other son, Tony who was attending college there. The three of us would then drive back to Toronto and fly to Winnipeg where Marlene would have just gotten off the plane from Regina to Winnipeg to meet us.

Got it all now?

Everything started according to plan. Marlene arrived in Regina to visit with her family while Cam and I met up in Toronto right on schedule. He and I drove to Erie to spent a couple of days with Tony, and then we three drove to Toronto for some sightseeing from our base at the downtown Sheraton Hotel. Then came the planned reunion of mother, father, and two sons in Winnipeg.

The morning of the flight to Winnipeg, the boys were in no hurry to get moving from our luxury hotel room. First, they wouldn't get out of bed. Then, they couldn't seem to finish their morning grooming which seemed pointless as neither one of them had any hair to groom. They both sported the youthful bald look of the then current era.

"You guys are flying standby," I reminded them. "We need to hustle." But my warning had no impact on their haste.

With minimal time to spare before our planned flight from Pearson International Airport, we arrived at our gate. I had a confirmed seat on the fully booked plane, but the boys were placed on a wait-list. Boarding for them looked promising but was not guaranteed. The boys showed little concern, but I rued the extra half hour that would have placed them higher on the list of anxious wait-listed travellers.

With the flight called, I boarded and took my preassigned seat while the boys waited their turn to be called. When regular boarding was complete I spied a dozen empty seats which would soon be occupied by the standby crowd—hopefully my sons among them. One seat filled then another. So far no sign of my sons. Two more and then another one. No luck yet. One by one all the seats filled, but none of them contained Tony or Cam. The plane pulled away from the gate with my two well-groomed sons left to contemplate their next steps.

Marlene met me at the Winnipeg airport as planned, but we weren't sure what to do about our two missing sons. Would they make the next flight which wouldn't arrive for another four hours? Should we take the chance and come to meet them? These were questions that Marlene and I contemplated as we sat in the back of the big black limo whisking us to our luxury hotel. We were treating ourselves well on this part of the trip.

The elderly limo driver seemed very kind and, we surmised, reliable. We decided that in addition to our fare we should give him a healthy tip and enough money for a second fare. We asked him to show up for the next flight and watch for our boys, whom we described in detail.

With the extra four hours, Marlene and I had lots of time to take full advantage of our large and empty hotel room in a manner that a couple might after a long absence from each other. We even had time to freshen up after.

Four hours after our arrival, Tony and Cam knocked on our door. They had just made the next plane. The limo driver had no trouble identifying the brothers as they descended the escalator at the arrivals level.

The rest of the trip came off smooth—other than the occasional scrapping of two young-adult siblings. At the end of the stay, everyone caught their respective flights back to their homes—Yellowknife, Regina, and Erie.

Poo-Poo in Poughkeepsie *May 1985*

My business trip was to take me from Regina to Toronto to JFK airport in New York City. From there, I would travel to Poughkeepsie and back to LaGuardia in New York City then to Raleigh, North Carolina, before taking a more direct route back to Regina.

My first hassle hit me at US Immigration at Pearson Airport in Toronto. Everyone else in my party was shuffled through by the immigration officials, but I got the royal treatment—royally shafted. When my turn came, the gruff official examined my driver's license (passports were not required in those days) and punched some keys on his computer. He kept glancing back and forth between my license and the computer screen which was invisible to me. Then, he walked over to a second immigration official with my license in hand, and they both stared at my ID and the computer screen. The first official looked over at me and pointed as the second nodded in apparent agreement. The first agent returned to the wicket where I waited until he finally waved me through. The ordeal never really jeopardized my travel plans, but it seemed like a long, unnecessary delay with no explanation.

I never found out why I was held up. The United States around this time was denying entry to some prominent Canadians such as activist Farley Mowat, but I bore no resemblance to the famed author.

The complexity of this trip and the tight schedule for planes and meetings made me decide to use only carry-on luggage. Although I had few experiences with lost bags, I didn't want to add any undue risk to this journey, which had already showed me its first hiccup.

At JFK Airport in New York, our group, all

using carry-on luggage, marched from our international arrivals gate to the domestic departures gate where our Poughkeepsie-bound craft awaited. Up until this time in my career, I had never flown on an airplane smaller than a DC9 jet, but this time I was in for a treat or not, depending on your perspective. I have never liked roller coasters.

As we approached the gate to board the flight, attendants informed us that the plane was too small to accommodate carry-on luggage, and we would have to use their sky-check service. So we all slid our carry-ons through a reception window for retrieval at our destination.

When they said small plane, I didn't visualize how small. By the standards of my travel in the Arctic, many years later, this would have been considered a giant plane, but the twenty-seater puddle jumper appeared to my eyes as a toy plane. All seats had occupants. Why were so many people interested in going to Poughkeepsie? I had never even heard of the place other than in jokes. I was only going because IBM had a production plant there that they wanted to show their customers.

A giant sat in one of the seats near the front. He must have reached nearly seven feet when standing up, which would have been an impossible feat on this sardine can. In addition to his unwieldy height, he was encumbered with a full-length cast on his left leg which took up most of the aisle next to his seat. Someone later informed me that this giant of a man was a pro-wrestler named "Big John," and sitting next to him was some dweeb affiliated with wresting by the name of Bobby "The Brain." None of this meant anything to me.

Other than take-offs and landings, I had never flown below 25,000 feet, but this plane, once airborne, almost skimmed the tops of the trees on the picturesque journey across the New York State countryside. If the plane could have flown at one constant altitude, I might have even enjoyed the view. But due to invisible wind currents on this clear day, the plane chose multiple random levels that didn't quite coincide with the natural rhythms of my innards. Cookie tossing came to mind, but I kept my urges under control. Looking around at the many green faces occupying the same metal cylinder as I was, I realized that I was one of the most stable passengers.

In spite of the ride, which was consistent with the "Wild Mouse" at the fair, we had a smooth landing at our destination. The twenty pairs of wobbly legs supporting green-skinned aliens descended the stairs to retrieve their carry-on bags from the sky-check cart next to the plane. It took no time for me to realize that my bag was not among them.

A quick check with baggage control confirmed my second greatest fear on this trip (the first was the fear of not surviving the Poughkeepsie flight). My bag had not boarded the same plane as I did. At this point, I envied the bag lady who had more possessions than I. How long before my bag would be located and returned to me? Not before my departure from Poughkeepsie, meaning that I was without a clothing replacement for my travel-worn garments, including underwear which I was certain had been soiled on our flight. And I was without my grooming kit. It also meant that I would not have my travelling tools with me when we departed for our return trip to New York City or before I boarded our flight from New York to Raleigh, North Carolina. This was the exact reason I used carry-on for this trip.

The airline provided me with their standard grooming kit, complete with skin-shriveling shave cream, a serrated blade shaver, a wire-tough toothbrush along with acerbic flavoured toothpaste, and a pocket comb with as many teeth as an elderly Inuit woman. Between scrounging from my travel mates and a quick trip to the hotel gift shop, I was able to secure some less life-threatening grooming tools. Clothes were another matter. The hotel gift shop was not flush with underwear and dress shirts.

The IBM sales manager who organized our trip offered me a change of shirt from his collection, but being four inches shorter and forty pounds lighter than I, this was a non-starter. Again, a couple of fellow travellers came to my rescue.

I'm sure my bag was chasing me for the remainder of the trip, but it never caught me until I was back in my home. It arrived by taxi about a week after I returned. The baggage tags indicated that it had seen more sights than I had. I'm sure all the baggage handlers questioned where YQR (airport code for Regina) even was. I have never relied on carry-on luggage since.

First in Luggage *September 1985*

Having arrived in Toronto for a series of business meetings several days ahead of Kent, my associate, I agreed to pick him up at Pearson International Airport in Toronto when he arrived.

I waited in front of the glass wall where I could see the luggage carousel spewing the bags from Regina flight AC 153. One by one, the passengers claimed their bags and left the baggage area destined for their rides or taxis.

Everyone was gone; the arrivals hall was empty with no sign of Kent. One sole bag continued its circuit around the metal loop. Ten minutes of watching the lonely bag convinced me that Kent was not on the flight, and I might as well return to the hotel. It was strange that Kent had not informed me that he would not be arriving.

Just as I began to turn, I caught a glimpse of a solitary traveller descending the escalator to the baggage area. It was Kent with a big smile on his face and a hearty wave to greet me. I watched as he pranced over to the carousel and claimed the only bag in sight.

With a big grin on his face he exited the sliding doors to bid me an alcohol-laden hello.

Before I could ask why the delay, he continued, "That's the first time that my bag ever came out before everyone else's."

I chose not to burst his bubble. I let him believe that he had, in fact, beaten everyone else out of the airport, knowing that he must have stopped off for some "visiting" before making his way to the exit.

Olympic Rip-off
August 2000

The June sun shone as I walked through Atlanta's Centennial Olympic Park. I gazed at the engraved bricks that helped pay for the park constructed for the 1996 Olympics. I recalled watching the bombing on TV. It happened at this very spot.

I barely noticed the distraught young, black man walking toward me. He appeared agitated as he asked if I could help him.

"Please, our bus broke down. I have twenty-five kids from our church in Memphis sitting on the hot bus. I'm trying to get in touch with our pastor back there, but I can't reach him. He must be on the way here." He held up a mobile phone to indicate his attempt at calling.

"Sorry. I'm from out of town. I don't know anything about Atlanta. Good luck." I kept walking, ignoring him as the fellow followed and pleaded. Finally, he appeared to go on his way and accost the next person coming by.

Just to make sure I lost him, I went inside the CNN Center. I knew my son still had a couple of hours of work before he could join me, so I just walked around for a while.

I came out of the CNN Center and saw the young man was still milling around the park. So I decided to just go for a walk and avoid him. As I walked down a side street, I saw he was following me, so I picked up the pace. He did the same.

He called out to me, "Hey, mister. Please, help me out. I've got to get these kids some help." He caught up and pleaded his case.

"Why not ask the police?" I suggested. A cop car was passing by at a crawl. So the young man waved down the cop car and leaned inside the driver's window to talk to the officers.

He came back to me and said, "They won't help. They said it's not their job. Please. I can see you are a man of God (poor observation on his part). Help me with these kids. Can you just loan us some money, so I can at least get them some drinks?"

I obviously looked skeptical, so he continued, "Look, our bus is just over there, off the freeway. I can show it to you. You can meet the kids. You gotta believe me."

The last thing I wanted to do was follow this guy to a location of his choosing, but he was convincing. I was starting to believe him. However, I tried another brush off.

"I'm just visiting my son here. I only have a couple of bucks. You'll have to find someone else."

"Come on, man. I'm desperate. Our pastor is going to take hours to get here. I've tried everyone I can find. They all brush me off."

"I'm sorry," I continued, "but there isn't much I can do to help you."

He was like one of those stickies on your hand. You shake and shake and it won't fall off. He kept at me.

"You must have an ATM card. Can't you at least give me a few bucks so I can bring some relief to the kids in the bus?" There was no shaking him off. I half believed him but half didn't. But I wasn't doing a good job of shedding him. He certainly spouted a lot of Bible quotes and was convincing in his religiosity.

I'm not sure if I was convinced of his story or just wanted to find some way to get rid of him, but I agreed to go to an ATM and take out some money. I made sure he was not near when I inserted the card and keyed in my PIN.

As I was about to enter the $100 he requested, he added, "Oh, and another $20 for the driver and chaperones." So I withdrew $120 gave it to him and tried to send him on his way.

"Thank you, thank you. The Lord will watch over you. You are a good man. My pastor will send you the money back as soon as he gets here. Praise the Lord for bringing me such a saviour."

I gave him my business card as he requested, which included my address and phone number, on the off chance that he was legit and would return my money. But I think deep down, I knew I had just paid to get rid of him. I never heard from him again, and I never saw my money.

Gramma's First Flight
1972

Gramma was in her sixties and had never been on an airplane. She had seldom even left the farm to visit the nearby big city of Regina. The family convinced Gramma to fly to Calgary to visit her daughter Dorothy.

We took her to the airport and stayed with her until she cleared security. We made sure she had taken all the price tags off her new travel outfit and that she took lots of bathroom trips before going through security.

The staff at Air Canada assured us they would take care of her. Regina has a small airport with few flights compared to larger centres, so we didn't worry too much once we had seen her through security.

Gramma waited in the boarding lounge until her flight was called. The pre-boarding call allowed her to board first as the oldest passenger on the flight. She showed her ticket and was directed down the ramp to her Calgary-bound flight.

She settled into her seat awaiting take off. Just before the on-board attendants were about to close the door for departure, one flight attendant approached Gramma and asked "Are you Mrs. Deck?"

Gramma replied, "Yes. I am flying to Calgary to visit my daughter Dorothy. She has been living there for several years and…"

The flight attendant interrupted Gramma's story, "Excuse me, Mrs. Deck, but this flight is going to Toronto. The Calgary flight is at the next gate." Gramma turned white, and her jaw fell open.

Gramma had turned at the wrong gate, and no one caught her. She was very upset and ready to call off the trip. But the attendants escorted her safely to her Calgary flight and correct seat to finish her journey.

The return trip went much smoother.

Patty Melt *1970*

"...She had so many children; she didn't know what to do." The old woman in the shoe describes Donnie and Shirley's household (my brother and his wife). They had six children, and the children always had friends around. It was a madhouse.

Donnie was one of the first to adopt the van as a mode of transportation for big families. Donnie, Shirley, their six offspring, and many friends piled in the van for a weekend trip from Vancouver to Seattle.

After a boisterous time enjoying Seattle, they started the journey home, tired from all the weekend activities. Too far to make it on one tank, Donnie stopped for gas at a roadside gas station just off the busy freeway. Everyone hopped out for bathroom breaks, drinks, snacks, and so on.

"Everyone in? OK. It's off again. Only another few hours to home." Shirley tried to keep the crowd under control. Then she went cold. "Where is Patty? Is Patty back there?" No one could account for Patty.

"Donnie, stop the car. We forgot Patty."

An hour had gone by, since they had stopped for gas. On the freeway there weren't many places where you could reverse directions. It was over two hours, by the time they got back to the service station where they found six-year old Patty in absolute hysterics as the workers at the gas station tried to comfort her.

No one knows what long term impact events have on children, but Patty did not grow up to be a normal person. Can her adult "issues" be traced back to this trip?

<<END>>

Note from the author

Thank you for taking the time to read my book "Adventures in Travel". I love hearing from my readers whether they be positive comments or constructive comments. I have thick skin so feel free to tell me what you really think. Reviews on Amazon or on Goodreads are also very helpful.

Brian Borgford

Email: brianborgford@hotmail.com

My books on Amazon:

http://amazon.com/author/brianborgford

33122133R00118

Printed in Great Britain
by Amazon